Take it From The Top!

ALICE WHITFIELD'S

Take it From The Top..!

HOW TO
EARN YOUR LIVING
IN RADIO & T.V.
VOICE-OVERS

RING-U-TURKEY
303 FIFTH AVENUE · 409
NEW YORK, NY 10016

Production: Mary Medland, Exactly Write! Production
Cover Designer: Evan Gold
Logo: Tom Chalkley
Photo of Alice Whitfield: Robert Simko
Printed by Thomson-Shore, Inc.
Dexter, Michigan 48130

International Standard Book Number: 0-9631048-0-2
Library of Congress Card Catalogue Number: 91-066985
Printed in the United States of America

Also by Alice Whitfield
"Ad Hock"

*This book is dedicated to
the memory of a man whose
voice lives in my soul,
my Dad, David Berman.*

Contents

Acknowledgements ix

Introduction xiii

Take It From The Top! 1

The Casting of Characters 7

Agents: Dear, Dear Agents 15

" '. . . Curiouser and curiouser,' says Alice." 19

What Makes a Great Voice-Over Demo Reel? 24

The Voice-Over Audition Game 33

The Voice-Over Session Game 40

Abbr. and Jargon 45

From Molson To Moonlighting 50

Putting on the Accent 55

Script Technique 63

How Do You Get from There to Here? 68

Hits and Myths 73

From the Horse's Mouth 94

Legends 145

Don't Give Up Your Day Job! 178

A Big Head Start 182

About the Author 203

Index 205

Acknowledgements . . . . . .

Over the years, I've written variations of my acceptance speech for the Academy Award. (Of course, I have never done a movie, but that doesn't stop me from writing the speech.) Oh, and I also deliver it every morning in the shower to the thunderous applause of my adoring fans. (You can create the sound of thunderous applause by cupping your hands loosely over your mouth and exhaling.)

I did perform Off-Broadway, but the show didn't get nominated, and even if it had, winners don't do speeches at the Obies. I have won some formidable awards during my career in the advertising industry. That's good. But, once again, no speeches.

So, here I am having written this book, and to my joy, I learn that I can write an acknowledgements page, my if-it-weren't-for-all-of-you-I-never-would-have-gotten-this-far speech. Although the cast of characters has changed, my intent has not. So, I'm ready for my close-up, Mr. De Mille!

To everyone at Real-To-Reel Recording, Inc., who, when not

doing the "reel" thing, read my manuscript ad nauseam: **Amy Ullman,** my partner and true friend (no, they are not mutually exclusive) who, along with her parents, **Jack** and **Rose Ullman,** have supported all of my insanities, including opening Real-To-Reel 11 years ago; **Jim Vickers,** the best engineer in the business, from whom I first learned the meaning of "don't give up your day job." **Eric Stuart,** casting director, who is clearly one of the naturally funny people I know. It has been a joy to watch him evolve. He makes me laugh. And he is also a big fan of mine. This makes me laugh even harder and that's part of why I continue to adore him.

To friends and relatives big and bigger, thank you; **Mitchell Whitfield,** my closest friend who also happens to be my son, hooray for you! You're doing it all. **Jo Foxworth,** a genuine pal with rapier-like wit, laced with just a touch of magnolia, has been prodding me to write a book, any book, for over two years. All right, already! It's done! **Milt Gossett,** an angel who has mastered the art of playing devil's advocate. **Nina Rubin Salkin,** a dear, gentle woman who is clearly one of the brightest people I know. Whenever I "hit the wall," I called Nina. Her demeanor and her four-year-old son, **Sam,** who thinks I'm "a very nice lady," had a calming effect on me. And, she's my only friend with three names! **Mary Medland,** my production coordinator, who has held my hand and my undivided attention throughout this whole "book" thing. **Sandra Choron,** who without ever meeting me in person, shared her time, her knowledge, and an introduction to **Esther Giller.** I am most grateful. **Mosel Katzter,** the most unlikely friend and advisor I'll ever have. He is one of the few people, under 30, whom I trust. **Mitchell Miller,** who enlightened me as to the importance of having a display queen for a friend. We've laughed—we've cried—we've shopped. **Roberta Silver** is my friend who, no matter what, just loves me! **Jeff Berman,** my nephew and

Real-To-Reel's former casting director, who possesses a photographic memory. Mine is failing by the hour. Already this is a relationship made in heaven. Through most of this endeavor he was my sounding board. He is also kind, and not afraid to be wrong. There are not too many of those around. **Helen Berman,** my sister-in-law, who tolerates my brother. **Birdie Berman,** my Mom, from whom I continue to learn the art (and it is that) of survival.

In getting to this next "thank you," I must say that although I am not a militant feminist, I am certainly conscious about the way our language tends to discriminate against women. However, my options of making the subject plural (and don't forget to pluralize the object, too!), eliminating the pronouns altogether in rephrasing, or using "he or she" instead, didn't sit comfortably with me, and it certainly did not read comfortably. With that in mind, my solution was to alternate pronouns throughout the book in order to create an atmosphere that reflects reality. I discussed this with **Michael Berman,** my brother the retired English teacher, who said, "For a younger sister, you're not so dumb!" Thanks, Mike. To every actor who has ever passed through Real-To-Reel for an audition, a booking, or a cup of coffee and a shtick cake: You are talented, brave, and I have learned from each and every one of you. And to all the people who have ever frustrated, angered, and disappointed me, my sincere thanks. I took most of that frustration, anger, and disappointment and turned it into positive energy which I used to help write this book! A special acknowledgement to my oldest friend **Marcia** who, along with me, remembers all of our teachers and classmates from P.S. 199, Brooklyn, New York, class of 1954, with great fondness and with amazing clarity.

Introduction

In May 1990, I ran the following quarter page ad in *Back Stage*:

WHY I WON'T DO YOUR VOICE-OVER DEMO REEL.
YET.

If you want to do voice-overs, I could produce a demo tape tomorrow that would make you sound like a million. But it wouldn't be worth *bupkis*.

Because if you got called up for a live audition, chances are you wouldn't be able to deliver what your reel promised.

I've seen it happen. I run REAL-TO-REEL RECORDING, INC. where I cast, write, produce, direct and record radio commercials and TV voice-overs for major ad agencies every day.

That's why I'm opening my doors—to give you what you really need—"hands on" experience. And where you really need it—in the studio.

You'll be in the booth. Behind the mike. On the spot. You'll learn your craft the right way, by doing it.

It won't be easy. You'll have to audition. And if accepted, you'll spend more than 18 hours over 6 weeks in the studio.

Look, I know you're anxious to get into voice-overs. But first come spend time with me and then we'll talk demo reel.

For more information, call me at (212) 889-1557.

Alice Whitfield, President

It broke on a Thursday morning. By the end of the day Friday, I was answering my five-hundredth call. That was just the beginning. Two weeks after the ad ran I was still getting calls, and these calls were not just from actors. Close to 50 percent of the calls came from people who were interested in learning voice-overs: people who have been told, "Gee you have a great voice. You should get into voice-overs." Men and women from many different professions (I'm talking politicians, engineers, doctors, yes, doctors, teachers, lawyers) who wanted to find out if they had what it takes to earn money in voice-overs. Many of these people felt that learning voice-overs could help them better deal with speaking in front of groups. They were right.

There is an intense fascination with this end of the business. It is more accessible than almost any other aspect of what is called show business. However, it doesn't get all the glitz and hype by the very nature of it. It is a *voice* business. There is nothing visible about it. You are anonymous. You could be sitting on a bus next to the person who is the voice of Anacin Plus—a person whose voice earns as much money from that one commercial as Billy Crystal earns for a one-night concert—and you wouldn't look twice. Yet, if you saw Billy Crystal on that bus you'd wet your pants!

The voice-over industry is open to everyone. You don't have to be an actor to make it in this business. Many successful voice-overs have never set foot on a stage or in an acting class. I am personally acquainted with voice-overs who began their careers as art directors, politicians, teachers, producers, documentary writers, and the list goes on.

Also there is more longevity working in voice. Unlike a physical appearance, the voice does not show age. It is almost impossible to tell how old people are by the sounds of their voices. It is an ageless profession. There are voice people who have been in the business from the early days of radio through today. This is over 55 years.

Just keep this in mind: there are more auditions being held for radio and television voice-overs (including narrations, cartoons, animations, and non-broadcast work) than for Off-Broadway, Broadway, and regional theatre combined. The general process of auditioning for voice-overs is fairly simple. Unlike theatre where appearance plays an important part, in voice-overs you are judged only by your sound.

Although doing voice-overs seems easy—I mean all you have to do is read from a piece of paper into a microphone, right?—It's tough. The talented people make it look and sound easy.

Memo

To: You, the reader
From: Me, the writer

I wrote this book for you—you who want so much to break into this business of voice-overs. You who have been told you have a great voice and should do voice-overs. You who feel it's an easy way to earn extra money. You who think voice-overs are a natural transition from stage and screen acting.

I have spoken to so many of you. And all of you have the same questions and the same gripes. How can I get a casting person to see me if I'm not signed with an agent? How can I get an agent to sign me if I don't have voice-over experience? How can I get voice-over experience without being called in by a casting person or signed by an agent? It's all one vicious cycle. I want you to break the cycle. And I believe you can.

This business, like most of show business, is *me* oriented. To make any kind of headway in voice-overs, you've got to be able to view things from the other person's perspective. You must be able to relate to them in terms of their wants and their needs. So, in addition to a lot of technical information, this book gives you insight into the professionals who make up the voice-over business—the agents, the casting directors, the actors, the agency producers, the agency casting directors and the writers.

Read it well. How you interpret and apply the insight and information will be the key to you making intelligent choices about your career in the voice-over industry.

I must tell you that it is very hard to make a decent living in the voice-over business, even if you are very talented and have a great demo reel. I'm telling you this, not only because it's true, but also because many people in the business asked me to tell you. It is also true that I'm not worried that what you read in this book may discourage you from the business. When you have a passion, you can't be discouraged.

One piece of advice: no matter what, always maintain your sense of humor. It will never fail you. I promise.

Take it From The Top!

1
Take It From The Top! . . . .

Voice-overs may have started with someone yelling out the window: "HEY, HELLO? CAN YOU HEAR ME? THIS CHICKEN IS TERRIFIC. IN MY WHOLE LIFE I NEVER TASTED SUCH A CHICKEN!"

Soon people began talking: "Did you hear that crazy person yelling out the window about a chicken? What's all this about chicken?" Quickly, word spread throughout the town and before long, there was a chicken in every pot.

Okay, so voice-overs probably didn't start that way. They began when radio was born. They were the voices that made their way into our homes through the air waves, the magnificent men and women storytellers with mellifluous, credible voices that kept us riveted to our seats, waiting, listening, believing.

In the commercial world, there are two categories of performers: the actor you see on the screen, known as the on-camera actor, and the actor you hear but do not see, referred to as the voice-over. Once it is established into which performance group you fall, there is a subdivision. When your voice is heard with a visual image, like a television commercial, it is called a *voice-over*. A voice is heard *over* a picture that is seen, a voice-over. However, when your voice is heard on a radio commercial, it is called just that, a radio commercial. Confusing?—Maybe. Tough?—No.

Besides radio and television commercials, there are other performing areas in which you can use your voice to make money. You can be hired to record non-broadcast voice-overs. It could be a narration for a medical film used to instruct doctors on a new technique, or one that introduces a new product line to a sales force at a business meeting. Audio books are other examples of non-broadcast voice-overs.

Another lucrative area of voice work is animated films and cartoons. There are people who make their living—and a damned good one, I might add—providing the voice for a cute, furry, little creature or some big, scary, old monster. Yes, it's a dirty job, but somebody's got to do it!

Governing Unions

The two unions that govern the voice-over and radio industry are Screen Actors Guild (SAG) for television, and the American Federation of Television and Radio Artists (AFTRA) for radio and some television. SAG is also the union for actors performing on-camera in commercials as well as in movies and television. Radio, television, and non-broadcast have different wage scales. The respective unions set minimum guidelines. In chapter four, you will get an idea of how the monies work in radio and in television. If you have specific questions about fees, contact SAG and AFTRA and ask to speak to a representative. He or she is usually quite knowledgeable and pleased to share the information.

The people whose voices are heard in radio and television commercials and narrations are often referred to as "the talent" or "the actor." "Who's the talent on this job?" "What time is the actor due here?"

A talent who does commercials is usually represented by a commercial agent. In most cases, the talent is *exclusive* to one agent. This means that the talent may not accept auditions or bookings (the actual job) from any agent other than the one to whom she is signed. The agent gets paid a standard percentage of every job the actor does. Who pays the agent and how much the agent earns are covered in chapter seven.

There are some agents who use *free-lance* voice-over talent, any talent who is not signed to any one agent. These actors are free to accept auditions and/or bookings from any agent who might call them. Although an actor need not have an agent in order to work, almost all actors do have them. A distinct advantage to being signed is that usually, when there is an audition, the agent gets the call first and, in turn, calls his signed clients.

Here is how the audition process works. Let's say the ABC advertising agency has to produce a radio commercial. It gives the assignment to the agency producer. That producer can find talent through a commercial talent agent or a casting company.

The Commercial Talent Agent

The producer calls the voice-over agent and gives her what is called a *breakdown* (not the mental kind). A breakdown is the term used when discussing the range of sound and style for each character and/or announcer within a particular script. At the same time, the producer gives the agent a time slot, a time when the producer will see the actors at the ad agency for the audition. The producer calls a few agents and goes through the same process. In a more informal approach, if or when the ad agency is not equipped to handle the audition process, the producer may ask the talent agent to audition some of the agent's signed clients right at the agent's office. Most voice-over agents have some kind of recording facility for just that purpose. Casting directly with an agent, in either event, does not cost the advertising agency any money.

The Casting Company

The ABC advertising agency calls a casting company and gives it the breakdown. Casting companies are never bound contractually to any particular talent or agent. They audition a variety of talent from different agents, possibly even some free-lance talent who are new to the business and do not yet have agents. Agents *are* bound contractually to the talent they represent. Therefore, they will recommend only their talent for any audition. The casting company then assigns the agents their time slots and holds a casting session at its studios. The casting company's fee is added to the entire radio or television production budget and is paid by the ad agency's client.

Once the agent is contacted, the agent "puts out the call." This means he calls his actor clients and gives them the audition. A call could go something like this:

Agent: Hello Kate? I have an audition for you.
Kate: Great. What's it for?

Agent: Dipsi Cola, radio. They're looking for a warm, youngish announce sound. The agency (or casting company) is ABC. Address, 123 Main St., 4th floor. See the producer, Bob. They'll see you between 12:00 noon and 12:30 p.m. tomorrow.

Kate: Great! Confirm me, I'll be there.

The agent calls back the agency producer (or the casting company) and confirms the talent and time slot.

The Audition

The talent arrives at the audition location, either up at the ad agency or at the casting company. She is given *copy*. Copy is the generic term for the script you read during an audition or at a booking. It is also referred to as a *script*.

The talent is given a chance to look over the script. Once taken into the recording studio she is given *direction,* an idea of the style in which the copy should be read and the tone of voice the client is looking for. She then reads the copy into a microphone. The actual taped reading is called a *take.* She is given a chance to do a few takes.

After the casting session, all of the takes are sent over to the client; the voice is selected, the agent who represents that voice is notified; the talent is informed that she has *booked* the job. In other words, she has won the audition.

The actual booking, the real recording session, could take place a week or more after the audition. It could happen as early as the next day. I've done casting sessions in the morning and the actual session that same afternoon. If the actor does not book the job, she does not get notified. It's an unwritten no-no to call the agent to ask if you were booked or if the client liked you. This is one of those times where instinct and common sense come into play.

Probably the most important sales tool a voice-over person has is his *demo reel*, a sample of his different voice-over styles on an audio cassette. A demo reel on *cassette* must seem strange. Why don't they just call it a demo cassette? Well, before cassettes, reels were state of the art, and the reference stuck. Anyway, demo cassette doesn't sound right. If a talent is new to the business, a demo reel can be created. A newcomer always has one created in order to get his voice on tape so that an agent can get an idea of what the newcomer can do. Think about it. No agents will sign you or even talk with you unless they have heard what you sound like.

Okay, now I think you're ready to read on. You will find individual chapters on agents, talent, auditions, bookings, creating a demo reel, and that's just for starters. Remember, so much of this business involves your common sense and instincts. Trust them both.

2
The Casting Of Characters ....

Where does a casting director come from? Does she wake up one day and decide: "I must be a casting director"? Hardly. It's not the kind of job you are born into. Scratch the surface of a casting director and you may find a former agency producer, a frustrated actor or, more likely, an assistant from the creative department of an ad agency who has been assigned the responsibility of dealing with and auditioning talent. Unfortunately, there is no formal training for the job. A casting director learns as she goes. The job is, by its very nature, a position of power and therefore easy to abuse. While many don't, some do misuse the position.

Where does the actor come from? Does he wake up one day and decide: "I must be an actor"? I believe that actor wakes up saying it every day. It is the kind of profession you are born into. Scratch the surface of an actor and you will find, not a waiter or a word processor—that's what he has to do in order to pursue what he wants to do. Scratch the surface of an actor and you'll find an actor.

There is formal training for this profession. If you are among the privileged few who are working in the industry, you are probably learning with every job. An actor must develop a tough hide to withstand the rejections, maintain a vulnerability, keep in touch with every emotion, and manage his business. The problem is, it's damned hard to develop, withstand, maintain, keep in touch, and manage, all at the same time. And while many can, some can't.

There is no explaining the person who becomes a non-actor announcer. This person never wanted to be an actor; probably it was the farthest thought from his mind. I personally know some who started out as art directors, producers, newscasters, and, believe it or not, politicians. These people can read the hell out of a piece of announce copy. While some of them can act, most of them can't read anything other than announce copy. The problem is, they don't believe that! The non-actor announcer will be referred to as an actor from here on.

With the above job descriptions, you can see why there could be lots of A&E going around, Arrogance & Ego, that is, and it's not limited to casting directors and actors. Writers, producers, and clients have it too. But this chapter is not about them.

Shticks and Stones

A casting director's arrogance can be triggered when an actor walks in and immediately presumes that the casting person doesn't know what he's doing. The actor then, as a defense mechanism, assumes a hostile attitude.

Quick, call the assumption police! The actor assumed the casting person was like some others, who don't know how to direct talent and who are insensitive. The casting person assumed the actor was a horse's ass based on her attitude. In a way, they were both right. Are there casting people who do not know how to treat or direct talent? Sure. Do some actors bring hostility to auditions? You bet!

Now, for the ego. You can be sure it will make an appearance when the casting director feels challenged. For example, an actor is called up to read for the part of the announcer. After the audition, (or even before) the actor says: "Look, I'd like to read for the other part, too." Or, "How come you called me in for the other part? I can read the announcer, too."

Here's nerve: The actor reads the part for which he was called in and then, midstream, changes his voice and, without missing a beat, reads the announcer part as well. In both of these cases, the actors are saying, "Hey, narrow-minded casting director, don't you know I can do more than one thing? I don't trust your judgment, so I'm going to try to read for as much as I can."

How about the actor who decides to read not only the part for which she was called but also the part of the announcer, claiming that women are just as credible as men, so she'll read the announce copy? Thank you, dear, for that bit of consciousness-raising, and right in the middle of the casting session, too! Timing is everything.

Do some actors act like that? Sure. Do some casting people really typecast talent? You bet! Maybe the nice way to get around that would be for an actor to ask, "I know I wasn't called in for it, but may I read for the other part, too?"

For the most part, casting directors are really good people. They're kind of caught in the middle. They can get flak from the agent on behalf of his client, the talent. They can get it from the talent themselves and from the agency. Plus, they get lots of calls and tapes from people like you who want a chance to be seen or heard. It can be hard to strike a balance.

If you do get up to an audition, no matter what happens, remember that the casting person is really on your side. She wants you to book the job. After all, she had the good taste to call you in, right?

Actors, Sharpen Your Pencils!

So now you ask: How do I get a casting person to call me in? Okay, actors, pleeeze, don't constantly call and badger casting people. It hasn't helped you this far, has it? Maybe if you send a spunky, but not cutesy, note along with your demo reel to a few independent casting companies as well as casting directors at ad agencies, something will happen. Here's an example of spunky:

Dear Casting Person:
Since voice-over casting is done, for the most part, without the client present, what could it hurt for you to read someone new? No, I don't have an agent—yet. I need someone, like you, who is willing to give me a try. The worst scenario? I'm dreadful and you edit the take! But just think, if I'm selected, you discovered me!
Thanks for the chance.

Give it a try. I've seen it work.
What do you do when you've sent a mass mailing to independent casting directors, ad agencies, and agents? It is now two weeks later—no response. Here's a classy way to handle it. Send the following letter:

Dear Casting Person:
About two weeks ago I sent you my voice-over reel. I am aware of how busy you are. Instead of my calling

you, would you please take a few moments, at your con-
venience, to fill out the enclosed self-addressed, stamped
postcard.

Your input will help me to define the style and type
of my voice.

Thank you so much.

Sending the following postcard is an effort that could pay
off. It is gently pushing the casting person to respond. Take
a look at two samples, one for guys, one for gals.

Guys:
Into what age range do I fit?
Teens ☐   20s ☐   30s ☐   40s ☐   other ☐
My sound can cover:
Real person ☐   Warm ☐   Spokesman ☐   Sexy ☐
Upscale ☐   Character ☐   Straight announcer ☐
Deep ☐   Other ☐
Comments: _____

_____

Gals:
Into what age range do I fit?
Teens ☐   20s ☐   30s ☐   40s ☐   Other ☐
My sound can cover:
Warm ☐   Sexy ☐   Perky ☐
Spokes/Announce ☐   Cosmetic/Fragrance ☐
Real person ☐   Upscale ☐   Character ☐   Other ☐
Comments _____

_____

Notice that I did not include a box that said I will or will
not keep your tape on file. If someone took the time to fill

out your card, chances are he or she will remember you and keep the tape. In addition, you may want to leave a space to indicate a return address on each postcard. This may take a bit more work. However, this way, you will know who returned your cards.

Please make sure that the postcard is self-addressed and stamped. Use one that will fit into a standard # 10 business envelope, so you can easily enclose the postcard with the note. Also, get yourself an index card box. When and if those postcards come back, you will be able to keep them in one place and refer to them.

What do you do if you get back some cards and on each one, a different description is checked off? This could mean that you are heard as having a wide variety of sound. If cards come back with pretty much the same descriptions checked off, that could help you focus in on your range of sound, how you are being heard by others. This could help "position" you.

Memo

TO: Casting people
FROM: One, herself

Whenever I see a list of casting companies, invariably it says, "agent submission only." As long as the actor is a paid-up member of the union, why can't you keep a list of free-lance people? Even if the actor is not yet a member of either SAG or AFTRA, each union permits a waiver, which simply means: This one's on the house, guys. And when the actor books the next union job, that actor must join the union.

In addition to calling agents to get submissions, you could refer to your free-lance list and call in some new people. And I don't mean just the students you may coach. This is a positive step all around. It gives new talent a chance to be seen or heard and it gives casting people access to fresh faces and sounds.

Let's admit it, from time to time we are all victims of the same syndrome. We rely on the old standbys. There is nothing wrong with that. They're great. That's why we rely on them. But that is not to say, with a little effort, we could not augment the list with a little new. So, what do you think?

Now, please forgive me but, on some occasions, some of us play God. If an actor gets to an audition 10 to 15 minutes after his call, we won't read him. If the actor wants to use our phone, we don't allow it.

True, there are actors who are consistently late for auditions and ones who have major "telephonitis." But we know who they are. And with a couple of choice words, we can handle them. Why should everyone be punished for a few rotten apples?

I happen to know of studios that post signs saying, "phone for client use only." Or how about, "talent may only use the bathroom in an emergency"? There is a casting company in L.A. that relegates talent to the "Winnebago." That's their secret code for not calling in a particular talent to audition for a month or two. This serves as a punishment for whatever and whomever they think warrants it. I think that's cruel. And so does the talent. But they're not going to come out and say it. That's sort of biting the hand that auditions you! Having been talent and having worked with talent over many years, I know that by being as generous as you can you're going to get the best work from them.

If an actor was late getting to your audition because his booking ran over, that's not his fault. If his last audition was at the other end of town and traffic was not cooperative, that is not his fault. Yes, I know, we have a schedule to keep and a business to run. But, don't forget, our business depends on the talent.

Although this memo was intended to be read by casting people, I thought it wouldn't hurt if you peeked at it.

3
Agents: Dear, Dear Agents

In the voice-over business, you must be concerned with commercial agents. These agents represent actors who do voice-overs, including radio and television commercials, industrials, audio visuals, and on-camera work in the commercial field. There are talent agencies that have both a commercial and theatrical department. Theatrical agents represent talent for movies, stage, and television. It is possible to be represented commercially by one agency and theatrically by another. Since we are talking about commercials, let's deal with the commercial agent.

The Agent

A good definition of an agent was told to me by an agent. The agent is a "professional middleman" among the buyer (that is, the advertiser), her agency, and the talent, the voice-over performer. What exactly does an agent do?

In that wonderful scene from "Tootsie," Sidney Pollack says to Dustin Hoffman: "I'm your agent. I field offers." Hoffman says: "Who told you that, the agent fairy?" Well, fielding offers may be part of what they do, but I think you should know what agents are supposed to do.

In an era gone by, the ideal agent was a nurturer, a scouter of new talent, a molder of careers, a star maker. But there is not an awful lot of that going on any more. There seems to be no time and no incentive to make the time.

Today, in the commercial field, it's the flypaper theory that applies most often. The more clients an agent can send to an audition, the better his chances are that one of those clients will book the job. But remember, this is just one aspect of an agent's work.

In addition to negotiating or renegotiating commercial deals, making new business contacts, taking breakdowns from casting people, and maybe even having breakdowns, agents receive hundreds of invitations from actors saying: "I'm appearing at so and so's. Please come and see me." And they receive thousands of demo reels, and certainly tens of thousands of follow-up calls: "Did you get a chance to listen to my demo reel?" And that's just from people they don't know!

Then, of course, there are the clients who either call or just stop by for I.P.B. (In Person Bitching): "I'm not getting sent up for the big stuff." "Ya know, I'm not all that sure I want to re-sign for three more years." And then the ever popular: "Why didn't you submit me for that?"

Under these circumstances, it's not surprising that some agents have what I'd call attitude problems. I should note, however, that there are some who have managed to maintain a good sense of humor through this whole ordeal of agenting. Some agents feel that for the time and energy they put in, they are not fully appreciated either by their superiors or by some of the actors they represent. Some actors feel that their agents are not devoting enough time to their careers. Actors who are looking for agents wish they had these problems.

Getting One to See You

So, the logical question is, how do you get an agent to see you, much less sign you? The honest answer is this: Short of holding a loaded .45 to the agent's head and demanding to be heard, it's almost impossible.

Perhaps you know someone who has a good working relationship with an agent, such as a producer, a copywriter, or even a fellow actor who is already signed. Any of these people could ask an agent to give you a listen. But, even assuming you're pretty good, why would that agent want to see you, much less sign you?

It's important to understand that, due to the current economic climate, which could change by the time you finish reading this book, not much new work is being produced. Agents aren't getting enough calls for their own clients—so how can they justify taking on anyone new?

And even under the best of conditions, another reason that an agent wouldn't sign you might be that you sound similar to a few of the clients she already represents. To take you on would be unfair to them as well as to you.

There are some agents who will free-lance an actor. That is, send him out on auditions without signing him to a contract, just to see how he does. If the agent gets good feedback or, heaven help us, the actor books a job or two, well you can fill in the blanks.

So, my advice: Call around and find agents whose policy

it is to free-lance talent. Oh, and 86 the idea of the loaded .45. Ten-four! (I love to talk numbers.)

P.S. If you do get an appointment, make sure there's a great demo reel in your back pocket. What makes a great demo reel? I thought you'd never ask! Read chapter five.

4

" '...Curiouser, and curiouser,' says Alice." ....

Fees

When you record a commercial for either television or radio, you receive a fixed amount of money for just recording it. Even if the spot never gets on the air. It is known as a *session fee*. When the commercial actually goes on the air, you get a *use fee*. Any time the commercial runs (is on the air) after the initial use, it is called *reuse* and the payment you receive is called either reuse or *residual* payment.

I've never understood why voice-over could not refer to radio, as well as television, since in radio it's only the voice you hear. But, hey, I didn't write the rules. Anyway, a session fee for a voice-over pays more money than a session fee for a radio commercial. And, a session fee for an on-camera commercial pays more than one for a radio spot or a television voice-over.

Still on that subject, the amount of money you get for use or reuse is different for radio and for television. It also depends on where the commercial is aired. If your television spot were shown in Iowa on a local program, you wouldn't get as much money as you would if it were seen in Iowa during the Academy Awards or the Super Bowl. Major programs like these are called network programs. They command more money because they are seen by more people, in part, due to the nature of the program. Makes sense.

Remember the two unions that govern all television, both on-camera and voice-over, and radio work: For most television work, it's the Screen Actors Guild or SAG, and for some television and all radio, it's the American Federation of Television and Radio Artists or AFTRA. I use most and all quite specifically. There are cases when certain television spots fall under AFTRA jurisdiction. However, at no time is radio governed by SAG.

Each union has different guidelines for working within its respective jurisdiction.

One wonderful aspect of the voice-over business is that you can do other things to earn money while you're trying to break in. But do keep in mind that in almost all cases, you must audition for any job you hope to book. These auditions are scheduled during the day: any time from 9 a.m. to 6 p.m. at the sole discretion of the casting person. Therefore, if you are serious about pursuing a career in voice-overs, make yourself available during daytime hours.

Actors are quite familiar with this type of schedule. Many of them choose evening jobs, like waiting tables or word processing, leaving their days free for auditions. However, if you must hold down a day job, see if you can arrange a schedule that might give you some flexibility. It doesn't mean you are going to be gone all day. It just means you can run out to take an audition when you need to and then come back.

Audition Scheduling

You can't expect casting people to work around your schedule. But, if you get called for an audition at a time that is really bad for you, you might ask the casting person if he will be seeing people at other times that day. This is perfectly valid because here's how some casting calls work. Let's say they are casting for a voice-over and the session is going from 10 a.m. to 1 p.m. Agents' time slots could be as follows:

Actors from agent A being seen from 10 to 11 a.m.
Actors from agent B being seen from 11 to noon.
Actors from agent C being seen from noon to 12:30 p.m.
Free-lance actors being seen from 12:30 to 1 p.m.

As you can see from the time slots, casting is going on from 10 a.m. through 1 p.m. This doesn't mean that you cannot be seen in any other time slot. Unless they are casting for different types of voices, and have scheduled people by type, I think the casting company would try to work around your schedule.

The Survival Mode

The most secure job I know is working for the government— and currently, even that is iffy. Anyone can be fired or retired. But in case you're interested, no one I know has ever gotten fired from doing voice-overs. If you are good enough and lucky enough to make it, you will have more longevity in voice-overs than in on-camera. Getting older is a more visual process than an aural one. When you listen to a television voice-over or a radio spot, it's almost impossible to determine the age of the actor by the sound of her voice.

There are some voice-over people who are doing a lot more than just surviving. Some have made so much money in this business that they have been able to invest in other income-producing ventures. So, when the business slows to a roaring stop, and God knows it can, you'll hear, "No big deal. It'll turn around. It always does." Sure! It's easy for them to say!

There are others who just seem to do well consistently. Good business, bad business, no matter. You never hear them say very much. You can't really hate them, because at least they have the class to keep a low profile.

And then there are the ones who want everyone to know they are doing well, even if they are not! They'll come into a waiting room filled with other actors, pull out the appointment book and pen, pick up the phone and carry on a very loud conversation that might go something like this: "Yeah, hey what's up? Another BOOKING? Well, all right, but I won't be able to make those FIVE MORE AUDITIONS. Call and tell them I won't be there because I have a BOOKING. What? Oh, it's a NETWORK* spot? With 17 TAGS**? Thanks, bye."

Then, Mr. Wonderful checks the room to make sure everyone heard him. All the other actors have their heads buried in the audition copy. No one dares to look up for fear of a repeat performance. This type of person is easy to hate.

Some actors are just plain honest. When it's slow, you may hear: "Gee, how is it for you? I'm way off from last year," or

---

*A network commercial can run on any or all of the major networks. It pays the best.

**A tag is heard at the end of a spot. If you do one commercial with 17 tags, you get paid for one commercial plus 16 times the tag rate. (Tags are discussed in detail in chapter eight.)

"God, am I dead! I've had one audition in two weeks. And that was for a radio demo!'"*

Some get some work sometimes but not enough work all the time. So, they don't give up their day jobs. When it's slow, some are lucky enough to have spots on the air and can collect residuals. When business picks up, they have nothing on the air so they collect unemployment! The whole thing doesn't make any sense—but hey, this is show business, who said it would?

*Demo is short for demonstration. A demo recording of a radio spot is usually not for broadcast. It pays a small one-time fee.

5
What Makes a Great Voice-Over Demo Reel?

If you are new in the business and are creating a demo reel from scratch, remember it must represent your sound, range, and abilities. To the voice-over actor, her reel is her resume. Eventually, it will be heard by agents, casting directors, agency producers, and creatives (writers and art directors), so it better be great.

What to Avoid

First, let me tell you what makes a lousy demo reel. Believe me, I know from lousy. People send them to me every day. Again, your reel is your business card, your portfolio. It represents you. So, don't look for bargains. Some actors get their reels done by friends for free. In many of those cases, they overpay! Others pay dearly, and the result is the same.

It goes like this: four or five dull and boring narrations that seem to go on forever, and then, for a change, a "cutesy" spot.

(Excuse me, this person should not do cutesy.) Directed by someone who should be selling shoes, they all begin and end the same way; they are post-produced with some glaringly obvious elevator music which, in fact, does not even relate to the narration; they are mixed together where the voice, music, and sound effects are not balanced; and then they are slapped together by someone with the sensitivity of cloth.

Okay, on to the good stuff. First, it's important you understand that the making of a demo reel takes time—at least one month, if not longer.

Setting Up Sessions

Set up three or four recording sessions with a professional producer. (Some hints on questions you need to ask when selecting a professional to help you create a demo reel are in chapter 10.) Schedule two in one week, preferably one at the beginning of the week and one toward the end of the week, and two more the following week. The theory behind this schedule is that over the four sessions your performances will vary, as will the sound, or ambiance, as it's called, inside the studio. This is good. It certainly won't sound as though you spit out all the takes in one day. Remember, a working actor's demo reel is made up of aired spots that were recorded and produced in different studios at different times.

Make sure to record more material than you will need. It's always good to have more. It gives you options. Record a couple of five- or 10-second I.D.s. (I.D. is short for identification.) In this case, an I.D. is a shorter version of a 30-second or 60-second commercial. It's good to use them for your demo reel. They help break up the longer pieces. No I.D. should be more than 15 to 20 seconds.

Selecting Material

The selection of copy is critical. It is also quite individual. Here are some general guidelines to keep in mind.

Copy must complement and enhance your type of voice, so select copy that shows your range. Variety of style is a plus. However, if you have a limited range, don't try to fake it by choosing copy that is clearly not your style. It isn't hard to pick out a voice that doesn't really fit the copy or vice versa. It smacks of a made-up demo reel, and a bad one at that. So stay within your range. Allow the sound effects and music to add variety.

Never mix commercial spots with cartoon or character spots, unless the cartoon or character voice is part of a commercial.

Never mix commercial spots with industrial narrations. Keep your commercial reel just that, commercial. If your strengths are in either the industrial narrations or cartoon voices, do a cartoon demo reel or a narration demo reel. Don't mix and match.

Post-Production

All the work done after the raw voice is recorded is called *post-production*. It's crucial to know about it. It's like understanding the surgery you're about to have. No, you can't perform the operation yourself, but you'll be better able to make intelligent suggestions and recognize the difference between good and better.

Assembling, mixing, and sequencing in post-production are three essential elements that add to the success of your reel. Of course, the ultimate success is booking a job.

Assembling your reel means putting together your good takes, laying in all of the sound effects and music. *Mixing* is balancing the sound levels of the different elements and transferring them from multi-track to either mono or stereo. A mono or stereo reel-to-reel tape or cassette can be played on most consumer machines. Now all of the elements are balanced and mixed down to one entity from which copies can be made. The *sequencing* of the different commercials, I.D.s, etc., is crucial. It's putting all the spots into an exciting, ear-catching order. You need somebody with a good ear and a good idea of what will work. Don't take on that responsibility alone. You are not the best judge of how others hear your sound.

When you add music to a spot, make sure it works with the copy and that your voice and the music start together. Never start or end with a section of music and no voice. I mean, whose reel is this anyway?

Try this: If you find that your voice sounds similar in two consecutive spots, have the engineer cut the very end of the first piece to the very beginning of the second piece, as close together as possible, without leaving any breathing room. This is called *hard cutting*. Tell the engineer, "Butt them together—no air." This will: 1) impress the engineer like crazy and, 2) create a contrast between the two pieces. If the pieces are still too similar, don't have them follow each other. Listening can be lulling. The technique of hard cutting also serves to jar the listener's ear.

Also, when you use a *fade out* technique—lowering the volume until it's inaudible on either music or just voice—keep your fades short.

Sequence the pieces to help achieve more variety. Try voice alone, voice with music, and voice with sound effects. (Not necessarily in that order.)

Keep in mind that the ear is fickle and bores easily. There must be constant movement within the reel. When casting people or agency creatives listen to your reel—you should be so lucky—the goal is that they should stay awake!

It's impossible to second-guess what casting people or agency creatives are looking for. Criteria vary from job to job. But it's safe to say that you should not try to impress them with the latest Burger King voice-over that you obviously did not do. Variety, pacing, and production value should be your goals.

One other thing—ask the engineer to *equalize (EQ)* your voice differently on some of the spots. Equalizing is an engineer's technique that can electronically change or alter the character of your voice. It can add warmth to your sound. It can make your voice sound like it's coming through a telephone, a tunnel, or even the Grand Canyon. It can even make one of your spots sound like a television voice-over.

The recorded sound for television is unmistakable. Usually, when an audio transfer is made from a television commercial, you can hear how noisy and tinny the sound really is. When you're watching that very same spot on television, you never notice the quality of sound. You're too involved with the content of what you are watching.

Television sound quality can be added to a tape with the appropriate EQ. In the case of your demo reel, this could be a plus. After all, without having to say a word, your reel suggests that you have done television as well as radio. Nice touch!

Dos and Don'ts

Keep your reel at about two minutes in length. It is most unusual for anyone to sit and listen for much longer. If your reel does not excite the ear right from the beginning, two minutes will seem too long.

The question always comes up: "Should I put my picture on the box?" My answer? No. This is your voice-over reel—get it? What if a casting person or a producer or a writer goes to listen to your tape, sees your picture, and decides he doesn't like the way you look? Maybe your picture reminds him of an ex-mate. Bottom line, he doesn't listen to the tape. Why risk it? Keep it simple.

Now, where do you go to get this great demo reel made? You can go anywhere and to anyone who produces demo reels for actors. If you don't know anyone who can recommend a person or place, look in your local trade papers. Just remember the tips and information in this chapter. (And in chapter 10.) Use them to ask the right questions. Make sure the answers you get agree with or come close to what you've read. The rest is instinct and chemistry.

Expect to pay between $800 to $1,400 for a great demo reel. That includes direction, recording studio, sound effects, music, mixing, and a 7½ ips mono master. *Ips* stands for inches per second. When material is recorded in a studio, it is usually recorded at 15 ips. The faster a piece of tape moves across the record heads of a machine, the less noise it attracts. It is then mixed down to either mono or stereo, at 7½ ips, the standard by which a home recorder can play it back. Cassettes only come one way. There are no ips problems.

If you can't afford to plunk down the entire amount, it would not be unreasonable to offer an up-front deposit and, to pay it off as you go or pay the balance upon your approval of the finished product.

If the person says no, go someplace else. Why pay in full before the work is completed?

You should know that *dupes* (short for duplications or copies of your reel) are made from the master tape, the original. If the studio that did your reel is doing your dupes, it already has your master. However, if you are having your dupes made at some other place, it is a good idea to have a safety copy made directly from the master. The cost for this is between $8 and $10. Keep that copy at the studio that did your reel. Then, you can feel safe taking your master elsewhere.

When ordering copies, don't go crazy. Twenty-five cassettes are usually enough to start. (That's not including the copies for all your relatives.) I mention getting cassette copies as opposed to reel-to-reel. Today, cassette copies are the standard. Almost every creative person at an agency keeps a cassette player at his desk. It's very accessible. You may want to order five reels as well, since some people still enjoy using a reel-to-reel machine.

Memo

To: Agency people
From: A former one, herself

Testing, one, two, three. (Is this thing on?) ATTENTION PLEASE, ATTENTION PLEASE. HAS ANYONE SPOTTED A MEMBER OF THAT ALMOST EXTINCT SPECIES . . . THE REAL RADIO WRITER?

All kidding aside. Today the young writers at ad agencies are brought up in televison and print. Most of them don't understand how to write for radio. It's not their fault. I think that's the main reason why there's so much bad radio coming out of agencies.

To quote one of the top radio writers in the country, Joy Golden, President of Joy Radio: ". . . Radio writers are a very special breed, with special understanding of radio's timing, rhythm, pacing, and an ear for dialogue. Radio production has absolutely nothing to do with television production. It's an art form unto itself. And the few people who are really adept at it were brought up in—or close to—'The Golden Age of Radio.' "

I guess to have been brought up in radio's golden age, you'd have to be over 40. Well, these days in advertising agencies, it's hard to find a producer and a copywriter who are anywhere near 40.

I know from experience that many agencies turn over the radio assignments to their junior copywriters—and those copywriters consider this a punishment!

Any agency with clients who use radio owes it to them, as well as to their young writers and producers, to have a radio maven oversee projects from concept through production.

This could be an opportunity for the younger crop of creatives to learn from someone who has lived the era! I really think it's time that agencies acknowledge that writing, casting and producing for radio are special skills that should be executed by those who have lived it—understand it—and love it!

Now, it's true that this memo is directed to agency people. But it's important for you, the person interested in voice-overs as a career, to understand part of why there is so much mediocre radio writing and producing going on.

6
The Voice-Over Audition Game....

It's the moment you've been waiting for. You've checked your service 20 times a day for the call. You have an audition. Immediately note in your appointment book the time, the date, and the address of the audition; the agent who sent you out, the ad agency, the product, and the name of the person for whom you are auditioning. This is very important, because if you're called back, you can greet that person by name.

Casting people and producers see so many actors that they may not remember you by name. However, if you find yourself back there auditioning more than three times, it's safe to assume they are asking for you, by name.

Sign In Please

At any and every audition, there should be a sign-in sheet. When the actor arrives for the audition, he signs his name,

Social Security number, his agent's name, call time (the time he was scheduled to be at the audition), time in (the time he was taken in to audition), and time out (when he finished). Why all the paperwork? First of all, when you get there, you are called in to audition in the order of sign-in. That's civilized. Also, it's for the actor's protection. According to union regulations, if an actor is kept waiting at an audition for more than one hour, he may request a W-4 form and be entitled to a partial session fee payment. Unless the circumstances are extenuating, I have never known this to happen. Anyway, it's good to know for your own protection.

Next, pick up a script (also referred to as copy). If there is none, when the casting person comes out, politely ask: "Excuse me (address her or him by name), is there any copy?" So far, so easy, right? Now, take that copy and read it, again and again. Make the words on the paper *your* words. Get comfortable with the material.

Marking Copy

No two people agree on the question of marking copy. There are some who advise reading the copy and then marking the stress points and underlining the important words like the product name, adjectives like delicious, fresh, new, smooth, etc.

I disagree. How could you possibly know before you even get in the studio how the casting person wants you to read the copy? If you underline or mark copy before you are given direction, you could be reinforcing the wrong stress points. When you get into the studio and the casting person gives you entirely different direction, you've quickly got to erase, unlearn, re-think, compose yourself, and give a dynamite audition. Good luck.

My advice is not to mark copy at first. Use the time in the waiting room to really familiarize yourself with the concept and the ideas. Don't try to second-guess the direction by marking words and phrases you think are important. Wait. When you're given direction, you can mark your copy. Always in pencil, please. And, whatever you do, don't forget to leave your baggage outside.

Check Your Baggage at the Door

So now you find yourself in the studio. You're nervous. You don't want to seem nervous. So you develop diarrhea of the vocal chords: "Hi, I'm glad I got here on time I thought for sure I'd be late you see I had to drop off my cat/dog at the vet he's being fixed then there was an awful problem with the train/bus/car I didn't even know about it until after I found myself right in the middle and I didn't want to be late so I ran and tried to get a cab what a mistake no cabs it seems some visiting diplomat is in town so certain streets are closed off so traffic is a mess."

Boring. Nobody cares about what happened before you got to the studio or anything else unrelated to the audition. Be a pro. Leave your emotional baggage outside. Come in prepared to work. Listen to the direction. Mark your copy accordingly. If you have a question, now's the time to ask it. If you see a word you are not sure how to pronounce, to avoid embarrassment just point to the word and ask, "How would you like this word pronounced?" The person will tell you and there you have it! Then mark it phonetically to avoid stumbling during the read.

Also, nobody cares what you think of the copy. No matter what you say, you can't win. Suppose you say you like the copy and the casting person doesn't. Not good. Or you mention that your 10-year-old nephew could write a better spot. That other person in the room, to whom you were not introduced, could be the writer. See what I mean? Travel light to an audition. No baggage.

Dos and Don'ts

On an audition, don't expect to do more than two or three takes. It is possible that each take will be directed with a slightly different focus. It's all up to the casting director. If only one take is recorded, it probably means one of two things: The casting person got what he wanted, or your voice was not what they were looking for. Well, it could mean a third thing—you were awful. Common sense should dictate into which category you fall.

When you finish the audition, thank the producer and leave. Don't ask if it was okay. If anyone volunteers feedback like: "Gee, you're really terrific. Where have you been?" Don't be afraid to tell the truth. Say you're new in the business and this is one of your first auditions. You might want to add, "And you guys really helped a lot—thanks!"

When you are in the booth and ready to record your audition, a slate is required. A slate is the audio reference that is put on a tape, e.g., "This is take one." At a booking, the actual job, the engineer slates all the takes. At a casting session, in addition to a number, the actor's name is also slated, i.e., 'Mary Smith, take one.' Some places want you to do the slating, others don't. To be sure, use a little CS (common sense) and ask, "Do you want me to slate?"

Don't use the waiting room at the audition (or at a booking) as your personal office. If food is put out for the talent, certainly take some, but in moderation. This is not your cousin's wedding, it's an audition. Also, if you need to use the phone to check in with your service or agent, ask. Then limit yourself to one or two calls, and keep them short!

Do get an answering service or a machine with a remote unit. Check it frequently. I have had bad experiences with actors who did not check in often enough. When you're first starting out, every hour or so, is okay. However, between the hours of 4 and 6 p.m., every half-hour is better. For some reason, things seem to fire up during that time period.

A casting person may call with an audition for you. He leaves word on your machine with a request for a confirmation. This means you should call back and say, "Yes, I'll be there at that time" or "No, I won't." If the actor is new to the business and is not used to checking her machine every 30 to 45 minutes, she may get the audition but lose it, because either the casting company has closed or it replaced her with someone else who was able to confirm right away. Confirmations let casting people know approximately how many actors will be in for the audition. By the way, agents are supposed to confirm their submissions with the casting people, too, as a courtesy. In case the actor can't make it, the casting person can call in someone else.

An important tool of your trade is a stopwatch. If you're new to the business, do not buy a digital watch. Get an analog stopwatch. An analog enables you actually to see time move. Watching the sweep while you speak trains you to see the passage of time and relate it to the speed at which you are speaking. Soon you will be able to recognize when you are running short or long without looking at the watch. But it is a good idea to carry it with you for an audition.

While some casting people feel it's not critical to come in at exactly 30 or 60 seconds, I think it's important always to try to read to time. Even though it's just an audition, it gives the writer a chance to know if the spot is over- or under-written. It's usually overwritten. Also, it lets the writer and the producer hear the way you sound reading the copy within the time allotted.

If, at the audition, an actor reads a 60-second piece of copy in 65 or 70 seconds, that slower read can affect the character of the voice. So, let's say the actor books the job. Now she has to speed up her read to make it come in at 60 seconds. By doing that, her voice can take on a different quality. Suddenly, the writer is questioning, "Is this the same actor we heard on the audition tape? She doesn't sound like the same person."

At the start of an audition, the engineer usually says to the actor, "Give me a level." He is looking to adjust the amount of voice that will be recorded on tape. Therefore, he wants the actor to read the copy with the same focus and intensity she would use during the actual take. So, don't just stand there and sputter useless chatter. If the engineer uses your unfocused chatter to set levels, when you begin reading the actual copy, the recording levels won't match.

As long as you don't trip over your tongue, read through the entire take. Don't stop unless you are stopped. If you've finished and are not pleased with what you've done, you might say, "It wasn't my best read, may I do it again?" For the casting director, it may have been the perfect take. Yet to you it was a "take from hell." In most cases, the casting director will let you read again. He may submit the first take, but out of courtesy you'll get a chance to read again. Don't ask to hear playback. Unless you're an actor whose name is a household word. It's not done. Period.

What to wear, what to wear? Let me tell you, I've seen it all. There are some voice-over men who will always show up wearing a suit, shirt, and tie. Some voice-over females are color-coordinated right down to their diamonds. But let common sense come to the rescue! You're new to the business. You are not established enough to walk into an audition wearing a loin cloth or a spandex mini-dress with matching sequined high-tops and expect to be taken seriously. So, dress like a mensch! Translation: Don't overdo. Don't underdo. To me, "overdo" would be an excess of jewelry: very twinkly, very sparkly and very noisy! And "underdo" would include shorts in the summer, worn by either guys or gals. I am hardly what you would call conservative. However, there is something inappropriate about adults showing up to work wearing shorts. Yes, I do consider an audition work—hard work.

7
The Voice-Over Session Game

You checked your service. You got the booking! You're at the session.

In the Waiting Room

Relax. Look over the copy. Wait to be called in. Sometimes you may be asked to do the paperwork—fill out the appropriate union reports, W-4, and production forms—before the session, sometimes after. Take note: on the union form you will see a reference to *scale*. Scale is the term used for the set minimum amount of money you can be paid. Scale is different for television and for radio, so a reference to *over scale* would be any money negotiated over the minimum amount dictated by the respective union.

There is also the question of *plus 10*. All agents' commissions are set at a fixed 10 percent of the talent's wages. When a talent records a radio spot, the agent's 10 percent is paid by the ad agency's client. In television, the 10 percent comes out of the talent's wages, unless otherwise negotiated. As I said earlier, AFTRA and SAG have different rules.

In the Booth

When you get into the booth, think of the microphone as a microscope. It exaggerates, makes things bigger. So, remove jangly jewelry, bracelets, and earrings. Down jackets or any jackets made with parachute nylon stuff make lots of crinkly noise, as well. Remove those, too. Put the jewelry in a pocket or purse, so you won't leave it in the booth and forget to take it with you.

Remember to turn off a beeper, if you use one. Imagine how annoying it might be, right in the middle of a dream take, to hear beep, beep, beep! This will not go over big.

While we're on the subject of extraneous noise, let's deal with mouth clicks. They happen when your mouth is dry. These clicks can occur within syllables of single words and between words in a sentence. The former is almost impossible for the engineer's razor blade to cut out. Under any other conditions, the ear would never pick up mouth noise. But, as I said, the microphone magnifies. So, when played back, those little mouth clicks can sound like a convention of Lilliputian castanets players holding their annual get-together in your mouth.

Nerves are the No. 1 cause of dry mouth. But certain foods also contribute greatly to the problem. Prior to a session, here are some foods to avoid: regular coffee or tea with caffeine dries the mouth; milk or dairy products cause phlegm; sugar, peanuts, and chocolate do the same. So, why bother living, right? An easy but temporary solution to the problem is water, just plain water. While you're glancing over the copy, grab a cup of water. This will keep your mouth moist and the engineer happy.

You'll want to take the water with you into the session, so that you can swish and swallow between takes. Warning: While in the booth, never place the cup on any equipment or on any instruments. Never. A good place for the cup is on the floor next to your feet. Don't forget to take it out of the booth when you leave.

Do you want to wear headsets? Unless you are recording to music, when it is necessary to wear them to hear the music, or recording to picture, when it is necessary to hear the on-camera voices as a reference for where your voice will be placed, using headsets or *cans* is strictly up to you. You might try wearing them for an audition—just to get familiar with the feeling and the sound.

The Committee

You're in the booth. You've got your water and your script. You are ready. Suddenly, your eyes move from the copy through the glass of the booth. You see what seems to be an endless parade of people marching into the studio. All kinds of people: tall people, short people, girl people, boy people. Who are all these people? They are the committee. This doesn't always happen, but, certainly a lot of times, it does. The committee is comprised of two factions: agency people and client people. This is sort of like the bride's and groom's family arriving at The Plaza for the reception.

On the agency side we have the writer and sometimes the art director, the producer, and the account people. Representing the client's side we have, perhaps, the client himself, between four and five other client-type people, and the various account people. And that's not counting studio personnel.

Sometimes a committee can turn a simple two-hour session into an all-day and sometimes all-night affair, complete with catering. "Who ordered the pastrami? Did they send the diet Dr. Brown's? I told them extra sour pickles!" It's important that you, the talent, remain unflappable and pleasant.

The next question is, who's in charge? My answer is, by definition, the producer. But the reality is it's "Rashomon."* Everybody's got a different opinion on how the copy should be read. Your job? Simple. Please everyone! Kidding aside, I'm not kidding.

It really should be the committee that directs all questions and opinions to the producer, and the producer who, in turn, gives you the input. Then, you make with the words. But it never happens quite that way. After a take, the producer can turn to the committee and ask them, one by one, "What do you think?" By the way, that's where the joke comes from. Question: "How many producers does it take to change a light bulb?" Answer: "I don't know, what do you think?"

Remember, while you are in the booth you cannot hear the conversations in the studio. You can only see faces. And sometimes, when those faces look disappointed and annoyed, it's easy for you to assume they hated what you did. Relax. In all likelihood the problem will be that the take-out place forgot to send the Dr. Brown's and the sour pickles!

Dos and Don'ts

Okay, so you do a number of takes and the last one is the buy (the take they liked the best). The committee loves it. That

---

*"Rashomon" is a 1951 Japanese movie directed by Akira Kurosawa. It explores the nature of truth, focusing on four conflicting eyewitness accounts of a murder.

means the producer loves it, too. However, you are a little less than happy. What do you do?

Some people T.T.M.A.R. (Take The Money And Run). Others might say to the group, "Listen, can I do one more, just for me?" No one will turn you down. After all, they have the take they like. What could hurt? So you do another take, one for you. And guess what? In many cases your take is the one they go with. Be gracious. Let them feel it was their idea.

Let's assume that your session was a re*sound*ing success (a little audio humor). If this was a radio spot, you might want to ask the producer if you could get a 7½ ips copy of the finished spot for your reel. A 7½ ips copy rather than a cassette, is always a better source from which to work, when transferring elements for your reel.

There are situations in which the producer might not be able to give you a copy of the spot. It might have been recorded as a demo. Some demos are produced for an agency's new business pitch or to introduce a new product for an existing client. In either case, the work is highly confidential. If the spot was recorded but is not yet ready to go on the air, the producer might not be able to give you a copy until after the spot is aired.

If it was a voice-over for television instead of a video cassette, you might ask for a 7½ ips transfer of the mixed audio track. It is the tape that has your voice combined with the on-camera sound and any effects, mixed down to mono. This tape will become the new element from which you can transfer a portion to your demo reel. You don't need a video cassette of the spot. Anyway, the video cassette is expensive. Make sure to get the producer's name and phone number. That way you can call and remind her about getting you a copy. It might also help to have the correct title and commercial code number of the spot. You did good. Go home.

8
Abbr. and Jargon .....

Not too long ago, I used my free-lance talent list and called in a male announcer. He picked up the copy, read it, and was quite surprised that he was called in to read for the part of a woman. I questioned him further, only to find out that he thought the abbreviation ANN: was the female character's name. *ANN* is the abbreviation for announcer.

Many inexperienced copy writers leave nothing to the imagination of the actor. They not only write the dialogue, but also what the character is thinking, feeling, and perhaps what the character ate for dinner. These references are usually parenthetical. Don't make the mistake of reading them as part of the copy. Other parenthetical indications are the sound effects. These indications become most useful in the post-production process. In addition to timing the actual dialogue in the commercial, the producer must allow time for the sound effects.

Abbreviations

The two common abbreviations for sound effects are *sfx* or *efx*. Besides ANN, you might see VO; this is one more abbreviation for voice-over, which is yet another way of defining the announcer.

Tag is a reference to the portion of the copy usually found at the end of a commercial. It may be read by a voice different from the *ANN* or *VO*. A tag can be of any length. Since it follows the body of a commercial (that's why it's called a tag), it contains wrap-up material, such as a phone number, address, and date.

In many cases there are live tags. For example, a radio spot can run 50 seconds, leaving the last 10 seconds to be read live by the radio station announcer. Tag copy is sent along with the tape to the radio station. The time of the live read is indicated both on the script and on the tape box. For example: Radio :60 (:10 live tag). This lets the station announcer know her time frame.

Another example is a 30-second television spot for a supermarket. The first 24 seconds are the generic portion. The last five-and-one-half seconds are for the live tag, which gives you the weekly specials. Tag information, either live or pre-recorded, is almost always short-lived, e.g., a price that is valid for only one day or one week. Creating a television or radio spot based on the short-lived information is not cost-effective. Within a short time the commercial will have to be taken off the air because the sale will no longer be in effect. Changing the tag information does not involve altering the generic or basic part of the television or radio spot.

Just as the tag is usually found at the end of a spot, the *donut* is usually found right in the middle. The middle section of the spot used for the announcer's message is called a do-nut—like a donut's center—because it fills in a hole in the music. Let's break down a 60-second jingle for radio. It can begin with 20 seconds of jingle with vocal. Then 30 seconds of jingle only, no vocal. This is the place where either the live or pre-recorded announcer goes. It is then followed by 10 seconds of jingle with vocal, for a total of 60 seconds.

When recording to picture, you might come across a script with the abbreviation, *SOT*. This is not a comment on your drinking habits. It stands for Sound On Tape. It contains all of the on-camera spoken copy, as well as the announcer copy. Sometimes it appears on a script just to show it all in context.

Jargon

Some jargon can best be explained by examples. Here are a few of the most commonly used expressions.

You're at the mike. The direction is to read straight through. You do that. The producer says, "Let's try another. This time with more smile in your voice." You do that. The producer says, "Okay, that was good. Let's do one more and this time *split the difference.*"

Translation: Do a take that has more smile than the first take but not as much as the second. It can be used in different ways. For example, "The first take came in at 58 seconds. The second came in at 62. So, let's do another and *split the difference.*"

The producer says, "Hey, that was great! That's a *buy* for

the *body*. But for the tag, let's do *three in a row*. And, make sure you *take a beat* between them."

Translation: He has chosen the entire last take (that's a buy for the body). But because the tag is so short, he wants you to read three in succession with no slate in between (three in a row). Take about a second or two between reads (take a beat). This is so the stop watch can be reset. Each reading is timed.

The engineer *slates*. You begin and make a mistake. The engineer calls a *false start*.

Translation: The engineer puts an audio identification on the beginning of your take. It is usually a number (that's a slate). Since your error was right at the beginning, it's marked on the slate sheet as a false start. You begin again.

The following terms don't need much in the way of translation: *Take it from the top*: Do it either for the first time or again, from the beginning. *Pick up*: Do it either for the first time or again, from wherever indicated. *Shave a hair*: Do it again, a little faster. *Lay it out*: Do it again, a little slower.

Here are two terms that you will not find in any dictionary. To get the full effect, I will use each of them in a sentence. "That was really terrific. Give me one more with a *skosh* more emphasis on the product name." Skosh: a little more, just a touch. "Oh, damn, you were off by about a *foofky*." Foofky: even less than a skosh, just a tad.

These last four expressions are rarely heard by the talent in the booth. The producer or the engineer usually mutters them out of earshot. Once again, a short set-up will illustrate.

The spot has been recorded and the talent is long since gone. The producer hears a little noise on the buy take. At that very moment, running through the engineer's mind is the horrifying prospect of telling the producer to call the agent to reach the talent to bring the talent back in the studio, assuming the studio has time available, to re-record and mix. Within moments the engineer realizes that in post-production he can raise the level of music or sfx to bury the unwanted noise on the buy take. It is then that the engineer reassures the producer: *"Don't worry, we'll fix it in the mix."*

The session is taking much too long. The engineer or the producer mumbles: *"Let's go. My car's double-parked!"* Or, *"It's getting dark out!"*

It's a music session. All the musicians are tuning up in the studio. The violin player bows an "A" on her priceless antique violin. The engineer says: *"Wasn't that tuned at the factory?"*

And my favorite: It's the third hour of what should have been a one-hour session. The talent is still in the booth. The take number is somewhere in the high three digits. The talent asks if the last take was okay. The producer grumbles: *"Don't give up your day job!"*

9

From Molson to Moonlighting

When a casting person gets a breakdown for either a radio spot or a television voice-over, it usually falls into categories. Take a look at just some of the basic ones. The selections are as extensive and varied as a Chinese take-out menu.

Straight	Deep	Hard
Warm	A/V (audio visual)	Upscale
Light	Comedic	Character
Sexy	Dialects	Impressions
Blue Collar	Real Person	Wry
Spokes	Gravelly	Credible

And, of course, there are also age ranges: teens, early-to-mid twenties, mid-to-late twenties, early thirties, mid-thirties, late thirties to early forties, mid-to-late forties, and so on.

Is there more? Are you kidding? What is not included in this basic garden variety is whatever is hot at a particular time, like characters from a new television series, a box office blockbuster movie, or a super successful commercial.

For example, when the television show "Moonlighting" became a hit, every other phone call I got was: "Get me Bruce Willis and Cybill Shepherd types." When the Molson beer spots were the rage, almost every copywriter was writing Molson rip-offs. So naturally I got calls for Molson-type couples. That trend got a bit out of hand. Even tampon commercials were written as if for Molson beer.

Oh, and let us not forget the *esque* types. "Hi, Alice. We need a Sally Kellerman*esque* voice." "Alice? We want a deep, gravelly type. A Tammy Grimes*esque* sound."

Clearly, they can't afford to hire Ms. Kellerman or Ms. Grimes—otherwise we would not be having this dialogue. Therefore, *esque* means, "I can only pay scale. But the voice should sound sort of like her. Not exactly—I mean with a similar quality—but not enough to get my *esque* hauled into court."

While we're talking about celebrities, it is true that some of them have incredible voices. Others are mediocre at best. A strong reason why the latter group is successful has little to do with the quality of voice. The viewer or listener relates the celebrity to his public persona. This translates into credibility. In other words, "If so and so says it, it must be true." This translates into big bucks for celebrity endorsements.

Marketable Sounds

Frequently I'm asked, "Do I have a marketable sound?" I always answer the same way. You don't have to sound like Orson Welles or Sally Kellerman to work in this business. But, there is one quality that you must have in order to work in this business: the ability to take direction. If I could bottle this quality, we'd all be rich. Sure, it helps to have a great set of pipes. But if you can't take direction, what good are the pipes?

It's analogous to buying a Porsche. If you can't drive a five-speed, what good is it? Ah, but you say, you can learn. Well, I say, some can and some, no matter what, will never get it. It is those very same people who, when told they are not getting it, DO NOT WANT TO HEAR YOU! I offer you my classic example of just that point. This story is totally true. You can't make this up.

Hello? Is Anyone Home?

A few months ago, I received a call from a woman whom I will call Joan. She was at a SAG seminar. My name came up as a source for creating demo reels. Joan called. After a brief chat, I invited her up to the studio to read for me. As I pointed out earlier, a great voice is not the whole enchilada.

A few days later, she dropped by. We spoke. I pulled copy for her to read. Cut to the booth. There we were. Joan inside and myself at the console, engineering, and directing, and directing, and directing. No matter how I directed her, she could not get it. She couldn't hear what she was doing wrong. She was like a person who is tone deaf trying to sing. She thinks she sounds great. This does not make her a bad person. When things did not improve, I felt I should sit her down and explain the problems. I did and she was very sweet.

Rather than just dismiss her, I invited her to sit in on one of my seminars. Perhaps by watching and listening to others reading and taking direction, she would get tangible criteria by which to compare her own performance.

Joan showed up at the seminar. It went along as it usually

does. The first thing I tell everyone when we get to the hands-on part is, "After you record, don't ask what I thought of your work, certainly not in front of the others. If it's important to you, see me when it's over. But be prepared because I'm going to tell you what I think."

Everyone gets a chance in the booth. They are given direction. They read. If they take direction, great. We do it again, only this time with different direction. Good. After about three or four students, it was Joan's turn. She was circus bad. To make matters worse, she asked me, in front of everyone, "How was I?" I reminded her of what I had said earlier, and she replied, "I know, but could you just tell me? I want to know."

I asked her to stay after class. I felt like my junior high school math teacher, Mrs. Levine, when I couldn't get one answer right in class. "Joan, please listen to me carefully. You came to see me. We worked one-on-one in the studio. I told you then that taking direction is essential and that I felt you were not doing it. You asked me then if I would do a demo reel for you and I said absolutely not. I invited you to this seminar. There was no improvement. Joan, in my opinion, I have to say, you are not competitive. I don't feel you will work in this industry." She thanked me very much.

Two weeks later, I received the following letter and I quote directly:

Dear Alice,
Thank you for letting me come to your seminar. I learned so much. I'm so happy you thought I improved. I'm looking forward to working with you. I will call you for my appointment.
Sincerely,
Joan

Listening. This business is about listening as much as it is about speaking. Listen to what everyone has to say. At this point in your career, you can't afford not to listen. Sit back and review the comments you get from everyone. If more than three people are saying the same thing—well, there is a wonderful Yiddish expression that means, if two people say the third one is drunk, he should go lie down!

In the beginning, it's difficult to step outside of your sound and evaluate yourself. If a few good people are saying you aren't competitive enough, go take a class. Work on it. If you hear a number of people refer to your voice as up or perky, maybe that is one of your sounds that appeals to people. So, go with it!

10
Putting on the Accent

In most of the world, an accent is an accent is an accent. In the world of voice-overs, accents fall into two groups: authentic and non-authentic.

A *non-authentic* sound is when the actor gives a flavor of the accent in either a comedic or cartoon-like way. An *authentic* sound is when the actor comes from that particular state, country or region, or she is well versed in the dialect germane to the locale.

A non-authentic sound is easier, so it stands to reason more people can do. Non-authentic sounds are usually used in a light-hearted vein. The focus is on the fun of the piece rather than on the accuracy of the dialect or accent.

Right now, I bet you could do a Southern, French, or English accent that would be recognizable and not half bad. Please, do not take this to mean that you should run out and add dialects to your reel. Not half bad doesn't compete in a world of great. There are those who do great dialects. And even when you're doing accents, you must be able to take direction.

The authentic foreign-born actor, who can do a credible read, is not so easy to come by. There are fewer foreign voice-over actors than American ones. It makes sense. In the United States there is not a big call for authentic Japanese voice-overs.

In our business, there are some agents who specialize in foreign voices. Some of the people they represent are foreign movie actors who have done very few voice-overs or people who have day jobs as translators.

As you would expect, there are certain American voice-over actors who specialize in dialects, even down to a certain region within a country or state. Nevertheless, in many cases the client will insist that we audition only actors born in the particular country or state.

About a year ago, we did get a call for an authentic Japanese voice-over. And as per the client's request, we put out a call for authentic Japanese. There were a few who showed up. With all due respect, the audition sounded like bad dubbing for a Kung-Fu movie. I knew the client would not be satisfied. So I called an agent and asked for an American actor whom I'll call Mr. X. Mr. X showed up and, because the client insisted on authentic, I slated the actor as Peter Akita. Yes, he booked the job. When a client does not understand particular problems and, in this case, insists on authenticity, he often gives up nuance and credibility.

Talk Good!

We all know that it's easier to put on an accent than to get rid of one. There are actors who were born and raised in many different parts of the country, as well as abroad, who have mastered the art of vocal disguise. You hear them every day on a variety of commercials. They seem to have no accent at all. They can turn it on and off at will. This is an important point.

Unless a spot calls for the voice to have an accent or regionalism, your speech should not have any particular slant. In many cases, it can detract from the message. While the listener is trying to figure out if the voice comes from Podunk, Boise, or Palermo, she has missed the message.

There are a variety of speech impediments that you cannot get away with in the straight copy and non-comedic reads. Only a few, however, can be translated to the page. These just happen to be my favorites.

How about the *ess* that sounds like air escaping? e.g., Do you have a sssssslow leak? And the *tee* that's pronounced like ts? e.g., Happy Birthday, tso you. What about the suffix *ing* pronounced een? e.g., I can't stay, I'm leav-een. I'm go-een. Get help. Go to a speech counselor. Recognize you have the problem and work on either getting rid of it or at least being able to turn it on and off at will. You want very much to earn a living in the voice-over industry—an industry in which your voice and the way you speak are what you have to sell—so you'd better talk good!

In addition, if you are aware of a particular regionalism such as a Joisey or Lon-gisland accent and you can control it during an audition, great. There are those who can do that. I hear lots of actors in the waiting room speaking with the proverbial "deze, dems, and doze." However, once they hit that booth it's a joy to listen to them work.

There are some famous people who have blatant speech impediments. Personally, I find listening to them annoying. But the majority of the public has accepted the lisps, lateral els, and all else, as part of the character of these celebrities. This only goes to reinforce the celebrity credibility factor. If you have achieved a degree of popularity, the public will accept in you that which in anyone else they might not. So, unless you are a prime-time news commentator, have a hit sit-com, or a few platinum albums, don't take the chance.

For those of you who seem to have a good ear for languages, there are dialect coaches who will work with you. Please remember, these coaches should work only on a particular dialect, not on the basic interpretation of copy. You might want to contact the United Nations, the language department of any accredited university or college, or a language school like Berlitz.

Before making that kind of commitment, you may wish to buy dialect tapes. There are tapes available for almost every dialect spoken. Check out the Drama Book Shop in New York, any of the Samuel French Theater Bookshops in New York, California (Hollywood and Studio City), Canada, and England, or any bookstore with a full line of foreign language material.

Voice-Over Classes

For those of you who have accents, cannot hide them, and still want to get into voice-overs, there is a limited market. But as I mentioned earlier, there aren't many good foreign voice-over actors reading for the American market. Perhaps you can fit into this niche.

You must take a voice-over class. This will familiarize you with reading copy and getting more comfortable with vocal nuances, colloquial expressions, and the basic disciplines of the voice-over business. Then do a great demo reel and send it out to all of the appropriate agents and casting people. As discussed earlier, in most cases, agents do free-lance foreign voice-overs. If you're good, you'll get work. Those voices are always a find. I like to think of it as being in a highly specialized area. So by all means, capitalize on it.

For those of you who are interested in taking classes in voice-over technique, which should not be confused with speech counseling, let me tell you that there is no shortage of people teaching it. Before you sign up with anyone, talk to people in the business and find out whom they recommend. Ask actors you respect for their recommendations. Also, check your local trade papers.

I caution you not to rush this process. I know you're anxious to get started. But selecting the right coach is most important. Whether you're calling through a recommendation or from an ad in the trades, ask the following questions.

Where are the coaching sessions held? Optimally, in a recording studio or a reasonable facsimile. How many people are in the group? Eight to 12 people is a good number. A group of under eight will give you more opportunity at the microphone but could be more expensive. If you're working with a coach on a one-on-one basis, expect to pay between $50 to $60 per one-hour session. Most one-on-one coaching can take place in the coach's home. This is all right because the focus is only on the breaking down and reading of scripts.

How long is each group session? How long is the entire course? A good balance would be a minimum of two hours per session, with the entire course running eight to 10 sessions. Or a minimum of three hours per session, with the entire course running five to six sessions. Prices range between $300 and $500.

Specifically, what is going to be covered over the entire course? Perhaps the most important question is this: Is an audition required? If anyone is willing to take you on without reading you first, head for the door. The one marked "Exit."

None of us is in this for charity. Anyone who cares about

maintaining professional standards will make sure a potential student can take direction. Taking direction is a prerequisite for learning the art and the business of voice-overs.

Although you will be in a learning situation, you will be expected to work on your feet. That's important. Always deliver copy from a standing position. You can control your breathing better. Ask any singer if she sings from a sitting position. It's almost impossible to control the diaphragmatic breathing that way. Some voice-over people record from a sitting position. For example, people with back problems, people in wheelchairs, people who record many hours of industrial narrations. If you fall into any of these categories, have a seat. Otherwise, get used to working on your feet.

Haven't I Heard You Somewhere Before?

There are voice-overs making a great deal of money from being very unrecognizable. Precisely because these voices blend in so well and are not identified with any particular product, they are used with great frequency. Make no mistake, when I refer to a sound being unrecognizable, it is not a criticism. It is a credible voice to which you attach no particular product identification.

You may hear their voices 10 or 20 times a day, for a variety of different products. Yet, you'd be hard-pressed to name the products their voices advertise. You would probably say, "I've heard your voice on commercials, haven't I? Your voice sounds so familiar. I just can't place the product."

Then there is the voice-over with a quirky or charactery sound. That voice can be interruptive in a good way. Much depends on how the voice is married to the copy. In special instances, the voice actually helps make the commercial memorable.

Here are some memorable marriages: Smuckers, Oxy-five, Hyundai, Gallo Wine, and Molson. In each of these examples the voice is identified with the product. Wonderful? Yes. Certain problems? Also true. If that type of voice is used to advertise too many products, the result can be over-use or over-exposure. I know you all wish you had those problems.

This is where a good agent is more than worth her 10 percent. An agent and her client together create some guidelines for advertisers and casting people to follow.

A financial guarantee. This is a predetermined sum of money that is guaranteed to the talent per cycle, per year, per anything the traffic will bear. This money is paid to the talent whether or not the commercial is ever aired. Some guarantees are against use, which means that the use cycle money is deducted from the guarantee. Some are not. You could call that paying dearly for exclusive use of a voice, and in many cases it is well worth it.

Let me explain the term *cycle.* Commercials go on the air for periods of time. These periods of time are called cycles. Some television spots are aired for 13-week cycles. Some radio spots can air for eight- or 13-week cycles. Even if the radio spot only airs for three weeks, the actor gets paid for an eight-week cycle, which is the minimum. Once these cycles are complete, they can begin again. Talent is paid reuse or residuals for another cycle.

Another way to keep a voice from over-exposure is through *geographical limitation.* The agent can decide where she wants her client heard. When an audition is called in, the agent must be told where the spot is going to run. It is then up to the agent to decide if she wants her actor to audition. If her actor books the job, the use of his voice will be limited by geographical location.

A cut-off date. The spot will run for 26 weeks or two cycles. That will be the cutoff. Having a cutoff guarantees that the voice will get limited exposure for that particular product. When the cutoff occurs, the commercial is taken off the air and the talent is free to book work for a competing product without the problem of a *conflict.*

The area of conflicts is also one of conflicting opinions. First, what is a conflict? A conflict is when the actor does a television voice-over for Brand X Coffee. If the coffee client says, "I'm holding all other brands of coffee as a conflict," then the actor cannot do a television voice-over for any other brand of coffee. However, if Brand Y coffee comes along and wants that very same voice-over to do a radio spot for Brand Y coffee, the talent may do so. Conflicts only apply to television, not radio.

I asked several agents why this conflict about conflicts. They all seem to feel that in television the voice is more identified with the product because of the added dimension of visual reinforcement. It makes some sense. However, in many instances, agents will hold conflicts in radio if their voice-over talent is already on a televison spot for the competition. Legally and technically, conflict is not an issue. It is strictly a moral judgment.

11

Script Technique

Although scripts, voice styles, and textures have changed through the years, what has remained constant has been the credibility factor. A voice that instills confidence and trust in the listener is credible and desirable. It's the real people sound, the voice that could easily be your neighbor next door, the pharmacist across the street, or even your best pal from college.

With all the new voices trying to get into the business, you'd think it would be easy to find the real types, but it's not. Something unreal happens when they get into that booth. Put a script on the stand and they begin to sell at you, not speak to you. People don't talk that way when they're not in the booth. Why do they feel compelled to do so when they are?

Over the years of working with people interested in getting into voice-overs, I have concluded that the hardest thing for them to do is just be themselves. People do not trust their instincts. Instincts, along with talent, timing, and luck, play a tremendous part in your success in this business. If you are feeling something instinctively, more often than not, you're right.

Hiding Behind the Copy

The booth in a recording studio is an intimidating and confining space. It's just you and the script. You must create a visual image for the listener with just your voice. That can be kind of scary. Many people hide behind the copy rather than getting into the words and making them their own. Hiding behind copy is what I like to call the have-a-nice-day syndrome. Doesn't it drive you nuts when people say, "Have a nice day?" You know they don't really mean that you should have a good, prosperous, rewarding 24 hours because they know you and feel you deserve it, but rather, out of habit, and for lack of anything else to say as a closing salutation, they say, "Have a nice day."

"Good morning. This is the I.R.S. We did not receive your check for the last tax quarter. We are putting a freeze on your bank account. Have a nice day."

Over the course of our lives, we've picked up certain habits that, when brought to our attention, are hard to defend. They are just that, habits. You travel with them. They've been with you so long, they're like old friends. More often than not, in the voice-over profession, they are your biggest enemies. They are vocal habits that are often triggered by nerves. For example, you may give value and emphasis to words and phrases in a script that you would never emphasize were you just talking to a friend. Suddenly, a credible piece of copy is made to sound contrived and phony.

When you pick up a piece of copy, it shouldn't be approached as just words on paper. It's important to ask yourself questions: "Who is my audience? What am I trying to get across?" And most important, "How can I personally relate to the message?"

All those questions for one little piece of advertising? You bet. I can assure you that the writer asked himself some of the very same questions when writing the copy.

The Moment Before

There is an acting technique called the moment before. When you get the script, read and understand it thoroughly. Then create a scenario in your mind about what was going on in the life of the person you are portraying the moment before you begin reading. Here's an example. The following is the script. The product names have been changed.

Ann: Did you know that Diet Dipsy Soda has no caffeine? None at all. But a lot of the other diet soft drinks do. Brand X has even more caffeine than Brand Y. And Diet Poopsie has caffeine. And sugar-free Dr. Hester has caffeine. But not Diet Dipsy. So go ahead. Try Diet Dipsy Soda right now. The only thing you give up is calories!

Let's break down the copy and find a moment before. Diet Dipsy Soda has no caffeine. This is big news. But what's more is the fact that many other diet drinks *have* caffeine. I bet I'm the only one who knows this. I've gotta share this with someone. It's too exciting. I'll just call my friend and tell her. "Hi, it's me. Listen, I have some news. *Did you know that Diet Dipsy Soda has no caffeine? But a lot of other. . . .*"

Create a situation in your mind that genuinely motivates

you. It works, it really does. Let's try another style of copy and another moment before.

Ann: The first time you wash with Super Beauty Cleanser you'll feel a difference that will amaze you. First, feel it soften as it gently removes make-up and dry dulling skin. Then feel it rinse pure and clean without drying even delicate skin. But most amazing you'll feel smooth, newer skin that looks fresh and more youthful. Super Beauty Cleanser for a fresh new face every time.

This voice-over style is "cosmetic-ish." Words like smooth, soften, gently, pure, and clean add an intimate velvety tone to the voice. It's sometimes called romancing the words. Think sensual, low-keyed — not low energy — and soothing. A bedroom voice! Imagine floating in a mineral bath. If you've never been in one, try to conjure up what that would feel like. No doubt it would feel pretty good.

The moment before: "I know you've never used this before. Well I have and you're in for a treat. You won't believe how wonderful you're going to feel. Close your eyes and think what it feels like to brush a feather over your face. The first time you wash with Beauty Cleanser you'll feel a difference . . ."

If you have difficulty relating to the subject matter, remember, your moment before does not have to relate directly to what the copy addresses. However, it should evoke the same emotions. Say perhaps, the copy is about having pimples, feeling embarrassed and uncomfortable, thinking people are staring at you because of your pimples. But, you've never had pimples. You have no idea how it feels to have them. Ask yourself: Have you ever felt embarrassed and uncomfortable about anything? Of course you have. So create the moment before using your personal embarrassment and then read the copy about pimples. You have just brought your reality to the copy. And because the moment actually happened to you, you were able to read the pimple copy with honest emotions.

Nobody can hear what goes on in your mind. (Thank goodness!) So use whatever you need to call on in order to help you create genuine motivation. There are actors to whom all this comes naturally. Others need to define the moment. It does not matter into which category you fall. If you are true to the emotions of the copy, your delivery will have credibility.

12
How Do You Get From There to Here? . . . .

Here is another situation where, although you will not be required to create a television spot or produce a radio commercial, as an actor you should understand the process. For the purposes of this explanation, I have omitted certain details.

The creation of a television spot usually requires an art director and a writer. With a little luck, they have worked together before and have created magic. As the concept develops, the art director commits his visual images to a *storyboard*. This storyboard shows the story of your commercial in little pictures. Each of those little pictures is called a *frame*. Beneath each frame is the appropriate on-camera dialogue and voice-over copy, provided by the writer, camera direction, sound effects, and indication of music.

When the client is presented with a commercial idea from the agency creative team, it is usually presented in storyboard form. The art director explains each frame of the visuals, while the writer reads the copy.

Market Research

If the client approves the concept, he may ask for some market research or a test-market run prior to any full-blown production. Testing is now almost routine. With the high cost of media and soaring production expenses, it seems reasonable for a client to spend somewhere between the $50,000 to $100,000 range to test the effectiveness of a concept, rather than gamble $1 million or more to produce and run an untested spot.

I should point out that there is no real proof that testing a spot guarantees its success. But you can get an idea of consumer appeal. In some cases testing is not done, e.g., when a concept already has been established. Then the agency will do a follow-up spot using a variation on the same basic concept. They don't have to test it because it has already been proven. When a commercial is not expensive to shoot, it might be more cost-effective to produce the spot without testing.

One way of testing a concept before shooting the actual spot is the *animatic*. The animatic involves actually videotaping or filming the storyboard and adding sophisticated computer graphics and effects to make it look animated, even though it is still. Since the visuals are limited, the audio track must be alive and exciting. It must help carry the enthusiasm of the message.

The animatic can be used in several ways. As a test-market commercial, it can be shown to the public. A target market is selected in an area where the product is available, and then the animatic is aired for a limited run in that market. This spot is known to be *airing in test market*. The effectiveness is tracked by the amount of the product that is sold or requested in that test area during the run of the animatic.

In the case of a *mall intercept,* an area is set aside in a shopping mall for testing a concept on consumers. A man-on-the-street type interviewer approaches shoppers in the mall. The interviewer asks the shopper to take part in some consumer research. If the shopper agrees, he is taken to a viewing area, shown the animatic spot and asked questions about it, e.g., What do you remember most? What was the product's benefit? What didn't you like? Would you buy this product? By asking enough people enough questions, one gets a good idea of audience reaction. This method is more of a research procedure.

A more controlled type of research is the *focus group.* People are invited to take part in a roundtable discussion. During this time, they view the animatic. Their reactions and opinions are observed via a one-way mirror. The focus group is told in advance that it is being observed and recorded. The agency learns a lot about consumer reaction right there.

Pre-Production

Everything that happens before a commercial is shot or recorded is called *pre-production.* Assuming all is a go, once the client approves the concept and budget, the agency producer calls television commercial directors and gets their reels. The director's reel is much like your demo reel in that it shows samples of his work. There are directors who specialize in such areas as food, beauty, or humor. The agency screens the reels and usually selects three possible directors. Each of the three directors is sent a storyboard from which he must cost out the job and submit a firm bid. That firm bid is inclusive of everything through the final 30 second spot, ready to air.

When the bids come in to the agency producer, he reviews

them with the agency creatives. Then the agency selects one director (plus a backup) as its recommendation to the client. The client sees the budget, views the reel, and the rest, as they say, is hysteria!

Radio, on the other hand, is a much simpler process. There is no art director. The writer and her pen make up the creative team. When a radio spot is written, either the writer reads it to the client or, even better, she presents it in demo form. No matter how much the client assures the writer that he will understand the radio spot if she just reads it aloud, he never does.

Demo, as we've learned, is short for demonstration. The demo is recorded, knowing that copy has not yet been approved. Recording the commercial to time is not as critical as it would be were it a final. However, as we've discussed earlier, it's helpful.

The talent selected to do the demo may not be the talent used on the final spot. (Sometimes talent gets ticked off because he did the demo but was not selected to record the final spot.) Creating a radio demo is done quite often because it is not expensive. In television you don't have the luxury of doing a demo because the cost is prohibitive.

Producing a Commercial

The average production cost for a 60-second radio spot, including casting for two actors, studio time, tape, sfx, and standard stock music is approximately $1,500. This does not include the talent's session and use fees, agent commission, union pension and welfare, taxes and handling, station copies, agency copies, messengers and media costs. That $1,500 average can escalate. Just add original music or celebrity identification and we could be talking $20,000 or more.

The average cost to produce one 30-second television spot, exclusive of talent session and use fees (in TV, agent's fee comes out of the talent's pocket), union pension and welfare, taxes and handling, three-quarter-inch cassette copies for the stations and the agency, plus media costs, could be $250,000— which can easily escalate.

I think because media, production and talent costs are higher for television, people tend to consider it a more valuable medium. For years radio has been the poor relation to television. Now, because of those higher costs, television has become prohibitive for many retail advertisers, so they are looking into radio as an effective alternative.

This trend is not limited to retail advertisers. Quite recently, I got my hot little hands on a media bulletin, distributed by one of the largest advertising agencies in the world, entitled "Radio—The Listened To But Almost Forgotten Medium." The first paragraphs read as follows:

> Most of us listen to some radio each and every day of our lives. We listen to radio to be informed, to hear the latest weather or traffic reports and to just relax and hear our favorite tunes. However, when it comes to recommending radio as part of our advertising program, we tend to forget about it. The purpose of this paper is to provide some general facts about radio and hopefully raise our consciousness level of radio.

HOORAY!

13
Hits and Myths

I recently sat with a group of actors who are very interested in moving into voice-overs. They talked to me about their perceptions of this business, and asked me questions. Here's how the session went.

You're in an agent's office. You got the interview. You read copy for him and he says all kinds of wonderful things to you, including, of course, that he'll call you. But, he never calls. If he's not interested, why doesn't he just say so? In the meantime, you keep calling and sending postcards until you're blue in the face.

This is not so simple. Maybe things have slowed down and the agent can't get work even for his signed clients. Maybe he didn't think you were as wonderful as he led you to believe, but because he didn't want to tell you that, he lied. It would be wonderful if everybody did the socially correct thing. If an agent sent a nice note to everyone who contacted him, he'd spend all his days writing nice little notes. It's just not practical, even though it's the socially correct thing to do.

You just can't take it personally. This is a business. That agent is not rejecting you, the person. It's a numbers game. Keep sending him cards, not until you wind up with writer's cramp, but every so often. If the business itself is awful, perhaps a short note that acknowledges just that might be appropriate: "I know business is almost nonexistent, but this is just a note to say I'm not." If business has picked up you could write, "People tell me business is good. People also tell me, so am I. Hope to hear from you." Your postcard might cross his desk just when he needs someone like you. Suddenly, bingo.

If I get signed by an agent, is it better to free-lance on-camera and just sign for voice-overs? Or the other way around? Or neither?

There are many ways to do this. Some agents want to sign you for both on-camera and voice-over. Some agents will free-lance you on-camera but insist on signing you for voice-overs. It depends on the agent. But here's something to think about.

Let's say a free-lance agent sends talent "Judy" out on a scale on-camera commercial for laundry detergent. Judy's voice-over agent, with whom she is signed, sends her out for a laundry detergent voice-over to that same casting person, saying, "My client needs $1,000 over scale per cycle." The casting person says, "Why are you asking $1,000 per cycle, when I'm getting Judy at scale for an on-camera?" In this scenario, the agent and the talent can come off looking foolish.

Many young actors have told me that if you have a very young sound, that is to say your voice sounds between the ages of 15 and 20 years old, it might be a good idea to free-lance in voice-overs. For that age group, agents do not have a large signed client list. Therefore, free-lancing increases the chances of getting called in by the different agents for the variety of jobs available. Some agents have started beefing up that age range, as the demands increase.

If I send my tape or picture to a casting person at an ad agency, will she refer to the tapes or picture when she has a casting call?

In some cases, yes. In others, no. Here's how that could work. Let's say the ad agency casting person calls the talent agent to get actors for a casting session. She might ask one of those agents to add you to his list of submissions. If a particular agent has a policy of not free-lancing talent, the agent will decline, and in that case the agency casting person can call you directly.

In another scenario, the agency producer has your tape. He calls a casting company to handle the casting. The producer asks the casting company to call you in. Casting companies can and should call in free-lance people in addition to contacting agents. But, in an all too familiar scenario, your tape gets thrown in a pile of tapes, never to see the light of day, except for the time when the casting person cleans house, and then it gets thrown in the garbage. Hopefully, if she somehow listens to your tape, and thinks you're good, you get called.

Should I send my voice-over reel to recording studios?

There are some recording studios that recommend talent to some of their clients, out-of-town clients mostly. So, it's a great idea to send your tape to studios. Since you are never quite sure to whose attention you should send it, either call and ask or send and guess.

Should you always try to stretch yourself with regard to your abilities?

Don't limit yourself. That's no way to approach this or any venture. Be smart. At the beginning, don't try to do too much. Get a little established. If they're looking for a voice in the late thirties and you usually get sent up for late teens, early twenties, excuse me, but where are you going? That's slightly more than a stretch. Going up for something for which you are clearly unsuited is casting suicide. I know you're anxious to get out there. Stretch yourself in class, with friends, and at home. Then, when you've tested what you can do and you get good feedback, go audition.

When do I update my voice-over demo reel?

If it's a reel you have done from scratch, there's nothing to update, so wait. The first real voice-over you book, get a copy and have it integrated into your reel. (See chapter five on getting a copy.) Notice, I did not say added to your reel. Your demo reel should have been sequenced for pacing. You should not just throw on another spot. It could create an imbalance. If the new spot is clearly different from anything else on your reel, find a good place for it. Since it's a real spot, near the top of the reel would be logical. If it sounds like something else on the reel, remove the something else and replace it with the real spot.

Integrate each commercial you book into your reel. Soon your reel will be made up of produced spots. From then on, follow the same theory. Common sense should tell you that if you book a network voice-over, you should put it on your reel. Because a network spot gets a lot of play, it's heard by a lot of people. Your voice is now more identifiable.

Do you recommend doing non-union work while you're trying to get into the business?

There are some well established acting coaches who suggest their students work anywhere, take anything, even non-union, just to get experience. I recognize that I am not a newcomer itching to get into this business. I am also quite sensitive to the passion, the seduction, of this business. Knowing and feeling this, I say you must set a standard for yourself and for those who are offering you non-union work by saying no. I'm aware that it means turning down work. Work is tempting, even if it's non-union. But every time someone takes a job outside the jurisdiction of the performing unions, it serves to weaken the very fiber of what those unions were formulated to do, and that is to protect you, the performer. The union represents you in case of any unfair practices. It makes sure you get the appropriate amount of money for a job. We are all aware that the unions are not perfect. Some of their rules and regulations date back to the invention of the wheel. They don't apply today. Because of this, a group of concerned, intelligent working actors is trying to make changes within the two commercial unions. It is not an easy task and it will take time. For you, for them, and what they are trying to accomplish, I recommend that you say no to non-union work.

Isn't it true that if you can do on-camera commercials, then you can do voice-overs?

Not even close! On-camera is a visual art. You use different tools—your body, your face, your hands—to express thoughts and emotions that need not be spoken. When you are in that booth doing a voice-over, who sees your body, your face, your hands? It is your voice, and your voice alone, that must convey the message. I have had on-camera people in the booth trying to use their hands and facial expressions to sell product. They are so used to the visual medium that in a lot of cases, it is very difficult for an on-camera person to make the transition into voice-overs.

What is a holding fee?

First of all, there are no holding fees in radio. Once a television commercial has completed a cycle, the talent receives a holding fee, which is not to be confused with residuals. This fee is for the period of time or the cycle that the commercial does not run. When this cycle ends and the commercial runs again, the talent receives residuals covering the new cycle, less the holding fee paid talent during the time the commercial did not run. This process continues until the talent and his agent are notified by mail that the agency has no intention of ever running the commercial again. At that time, the talent is said to be released from the spot and the client is no longer holding a conflict.

In another scenario, the television spot is running on and off for a year, on with residuals, off with holding fees. The agency has every intention of running the spot over the next year. But now the talent and his agent feel he should be getting more money for the spot. After all, the conflict is preventing him from other work in that category. So, the agent informs the ad agency that the contract period is up and they should talk about renegotiations. Renegotiations could involve any of the following: more money or a guarantee, a cut-off, or geographical limitations. The agency can agree to the requests or not. If not, the talent either backs down on his requests or the agency replaces his voice with a different voice-over who will work for scale. Then, chances are, after the new talent's contract expires, the whole thing starts again.

I get so down on myself. It just seems like rejection after rejection. How am I ever going to do it? How do other young people get by?

There was an insightful article in the July 13, 1990 issue of *Back Stage*, written by the actress Barbara Sarbin. It's called, "In the Wings? There's More to Do Than Wait: How to Make the Most of Your Time Between Jobs." Barbara interviewed six young actors. Each discussed how he or she handles his or her down time, professional and personal needs, mental attitude, getting from one day to the next, and getting through the frustrations. With the kind permission of *Back Stage* and Barbara Sarbin, I've included the article.

There is nothing worse for an actor than waiting for the next job to appear. How different actors approach this "in-between" time is highly individual. *Back Stage* interviewed several actors to see how they deal with being out of work. What we heard repeatedly is that there will always be times when one is out of work, feeling as if he or she can't even get arrested. Whether these dry periods last for a few weeks or six months, everyone goes through a panic: Will I ever work again? Is this worth it? Should I be doing something else with my life?

What follows are the philosophies of seven different New York actors, all of whom are professional, working performers, most of whom were between jobs when interviewed. While each one has a different method for keeping on track, there are several points they all touch on. One is that you have to be sure at all times that acting is what you want to do more than anything in the world; another is that being out of work comes with the territory of being an actor; and finally, what you do during those times is an entirely creative, individual decision.

Gabrielle Carteris

Theatre: *George St. Theatre, Perry St. Theatre, Ensemble Studio Theatre, Fulton Opera House, O'Neill Theatre Conference.* TV: *"Beverly Hills High," "Seasonal Differences," "What if I'm Gay," "Another World."* Film: *"Jacknife."*

Gabrielle Carteris has been working professionally for four years. When things are slow, Gabrielle makes sure she always has something to do, whether concentrating on acting classes, going to see agencies, following up on phone calls, or coaching actors. She tries to focus on what would be the most productive thing for her to do at that moment. "When I'm busy," she says, "I don't have time to do certain things, so when I'm not busy, I'm busy doing those things. I try to learn to enjoy that time off. I make plans with friends. I think the idea is not to make acting your life, but to have it be a part of your life." Gabrielle emphasizes that to really progress, one has to accept that acting is a business and to approach it that way. "And," she adds, "you can't bring your business home all the time. Have a life, have friends, don't have the only thing in your life be your work."

She admits that being out of work can get her down, she wonders if she's ever going to work again, or if the situation is reflective of past work she's done. But she has learned to step back and say, "All actors go through this syndrome. Even the most famous actors talk about that time when it's 'downtime,' and I think the key is to look at that time off as an opportunity." She finds it helpful to write in a journal; to acknowledge and accept that she's going through this phase again, and to try to observe her position, rather than letting it build on itself.

She also works out at a health club every day, because it keeps her mentally and physically fit, and balanced. "I keep functioning. I think you have to look at it as if you're on a road going from A to Z and there's B, C, D and everything else in between." She finds it equally important, if she's lost out on a job, to work at letting go of it, and to learn from the experience. She turns it around, focuses on what she got out of it, instead of being consumed by the loss. "I look at it like, how great that I went that far. I try just to see that it's all really part of the process."

To frustrated actors she has this to say: "This is a time to really make the choice: 'Am I going to stay in the profession? And if I stay, am I going to make it something that really means something, that's really worthwhile, and adds to me as a person?' You have to question whether it's worth it to be in the business. And you have to realize that this business is a game. If there was a nuclear war or something, this business would be meaningless. That doesn't mean that you shouldn't be dedicated, but keep your perspective."

If you've been out of work for a while, Gabrielle thinks it's important to use the time "to reflect and not to judge." She recommends taking classes, doing showcases, and handling business. "Get feedback when you go on auditions. If the feedback is, 'You're great, just not right,' then take that for what it is and keep reaching. The thing is, if you're liked and people are responding to you, then it's just a matter of time. It's just a roll of the dice. One aspect of this business is luck, and you have to accept that. It's not something that you can control, no matter how talented you are. It's not a reflection of who you are; it's not a judgment. It's not that you're not good or not attractive, it's something that's outside of you."

Gabrielle is emphatic about an actor's willingness to take non-acting work. "I think that an actor who's struggling and has no money, but doesn't want to work outside the business, is a fool. This world has too much to offer. If actors are denying themselves the opportunity to participate in this world, saying that they can't, then they're lying to themselves and I have no respect for them. If you don't want to make money, then go out and volunteer to work at a hospital. You're going to be a better actor if you participate in the world, because theatre is about the world and people. So if you're not participating, you're not taking in, you're not expanding, and you can't bring it to your work."

Richard Topol
Theatre: *"Carbondale Dreams," "Hyde in Hollywood,"* Long Wharf,
Playwrights Horizons, WPA, Ensemble Studio Theatre. TV: *"American
Playhouse's 'Hyde in Hollywood.' "*

Richard Topol has been acting professionally since he finished
NYU graduate school, two-and-a-half years ago. When he's out
of work, he collects unemployment or does word processing,
performs in showcases and student films, and spends time
with friends.

Rich talks about a time when he was out of work for six
months. He says that the big issue for him was one of self-
definition: "Who am I? Am I a person who is acting once in
a while? Am I a person who wants to be an actor? Am I an
unemployed actor? For me it was very important to think of
myself as an actor. I wasn't a waiter/actor. I wasn't an actor
filling in time with another job. I was an actor. I needed that
self-confidence." There were weeks at a time when he couldn't
get an audition, much less a job—but he was still thinking of
himself as an actor. He collected unemployment so that he
could concentrate on looking for acting work and so that he
wouldn't have the stress about worrying over rent and bills.
During that time, he says he chose to live below his means.

Rich concedes this was a time of depression, fraught with
feelings of inadequacy and uselessness, but he refused to
doubt his career-choice. Instead, he set goals like, "I want to
be in an Off-Broadway show by the time I'm 25, I want to be
on Broadway by the time I'm 30. These were arbitrary goals
that I felt would motivate me in some way, and also be a mea-
sure of how well I was doing. They were quite reasonable. I
met that first goal later than year and I felt good. I felt I had
succeeded and that gave me a kind of confidence and a sense
of the longer perspective."

Rich says it helps to keep in touch with people who are experiencing the same thing, and to talk to actors who have been in the business for years, to get some guidance. "Try to understand the nature of the experience, which is that you work, and then you don't work. Then figure out how much stamina you have, and how much you need to work to make you feel like you can still do it."

To fulfill your artistic needs, he recommends working on student films. "They're always looking for people and if you have any interest at all, there's a lot to be learned, and you get a tape of the film." He also suggests working as an assistant director, helping with casting, doing readings, and showcases, all of which allow you to meet people and can lead to jobs later on. Showcases especially connect an actor with the theatre world, even though there's no pay. Rich says it was extremely helpful to keep telling agents, "Oh, now I'm in something else," even if just to assure that his name was floating around anywhere outside his own apartment.

He suggests using such free time to see movies and read novels. He also sees a lot of value in spending time with friends when out of work, because it helps to combat all the self involvement. "My friends have interesting lives that I can learn about. I figure, I live in the world, and one of the challenges of living in the world is figuring out who you are and what's going on around you."

Rich also highly recommends finding a way to take an inexpensive vacation. He describes a week he took off, far from New York City, with tremendous enthusiasm: "It's great just to get away from it all. I was enjoying life completely. Life was a pleasure. Life wasn't an endless mixture of fear, apprehension, and a feeling of being out of it and useless. It was a new experience that broadened my perspective, opened me up and made me feel like I was learning things. I was accepting a whole new experience instead of being in the same old rut, the same old day-to-day grind. And when I came back, I had a burst of energy. I had something stored up that gave me confidence in being alive."

Julie Cohen

Theatre: *"Bring Back Birdie," "You're a Good Man, Charlie Brown."* TV: *"It's No Crush I'm in Love."* Film: *"Once Upon a Time in America."* Voiceovers: *Laughing Cow, A&P, Burger King.*

Julie Cohen was born and raised in New York, and started acting professionally when she was ten years old.

Because Julie does voiceovers pretty consistently she is lucky enough to have the free time to do acting work that doesn't pay any money. It's important to her to keep working all the time, to always have a project that she cares about. "I can't make the focus of my work getting work. I do as much of that as I can. But my work as an actor is working as an actor, not finding work as an actor. I have a lot of faith that if I keep working, more will come to me."

Even still, she gets frustrated. "Don't we all? The worst times are when you go and see a film or a play and you see some part you could do, and think, 'Not only did I not get cast in this, I didn't even get an audition!'" But she thinks it's vital to recognize that there's only a certain amount that's within your control. An actor can stay in touch with agents, send them flyers, ask to be submitted for certain projects, and do his or her best at auditions. "If I have a good audition, I've done my job. I've done what I'm supposed to do, and then it's out of my hands. I don't kick myself after every audition. If I were to kick myself for everything I didn't get, I would have such a black and blue behind."

There are times when Julie wonders why she stays in this profession, whether she couldn't do something more useful for the world at large. But then she thinks about what else she would do, and she knows the answer: "This is all I've ever known how to do, it's all I've ever wanted to do. There are times when I get frustrated, but I've never felt like I should hang it all up. I feel like it's so much a matter of timing—so much is out of my control, that if I were to give it up, I'd always feel like it was right around the corner." But, she adds with a comic twist, "I may feel differently when I'm forty."

She also tries to make sure that she doesn't do commercials that go against her principles, and if she has an opportunity to put out a message, she takes it. "I don't do anything for the army or the government, and I've argued with my agents about that. I know vegetarians who won't work for Burger King." Sometimes though, it's a question of compromising values for the money, and there's no room for guilt. After all, "You have to pay your rent."

What about those times when she has no commercial work even to sustain her? "When I'm feeling like I'm ugly and fat, nobody likes me, I can't get cast in anything. I remember that last time I got cast in something, I remember the last time someone said to me on the phone, 'You got the part,' or I remember the last time I took a bow for an appreciative audience. I remember that and I hold those moments like treasures, like jewels, and that reminds me that I'm doing this for a reason and I have a right to be doing what I'm doing."

If you're out of work, Julie recommends going to see movies. " 'Miracle Worker'—Anne Bancroft in the 'Miracle Worker.' It gets me every single time." She gets her inspiration from watching actors work, and goes to see as many plays as she can. "I am not into this competitive thing with actors. For me, we're all in this together, and I feel nothing but support for actors that I think are good and that I see working. I know I could be doing what they're doing, and it's just a question of getting there." She also suggests acting in student films, doing cabaret, taking acting classes, producing showcases, and attending as many auditions as possible, because for however long those auditions last, an actor has the chance to perform for a captive audience. She sees nothing wrong in taking non-acting work, but emphasizes that one has to remember at all times it's an interim job. "Go, work, make your money, do your thing, but don't get emotionally involved, and don't start taking your problems home with you. This is not your career, this is not what you want to do, this is to sustain you."

Judy Sternlight
Theatre: *Cincinnati Playhouse, NJ Shakespeare Festival, Cab Theatre Company, Wooden Horse Theatre Co., Chelsea Theatre, Prov. Duh, Some Assembly Required.*

Judy Sternlight has spent five years as a professional actor. During the last few years she has held a full-time office job in addition to acting in showcases, writing plays, and performing with improv groups.

Judy talks about how her work as a temp between acting gigs slipped into a full-time job and created a lot of problems for her. "I felt like I was not able to go to auditions, and I didn't have the freedom I needed. I was doing theatre after work, but it just wasn't the same thing." Now she does freelance public relations work in which she makes her own schedule. "But I still resent having to do something else to make money."

Even when she's not able to get a paid acting job, Judy believes that there's always something to be done that is creative and positive. "There's business, which involves sending stuff out, being aggressive, going to open calls, networking." When that gets frustrating, Judy counters her auditioning by doing her own writing and performing improv in clubs and cabarets. She finds this work fuels her creativity and her self-confidence.

Still, she makes sure she sends out pictures and resumes, keeps in touch with agents through postcards, and makes it to open calls. "That's my philosophy," she says, "There's always something that is achievable, and if you look at it that way instead of letting it overwhelm you, then you can really keep taking steps to get there."

Part of what enables Judy to keep going is learning how to deflect any feelings of rejection. "A lot of times what I try to do is breathe and say, 'Let it go, there's nothing I can do about what those other people think right now.' All I can deal with is what I think and what I believe. And just by taking action and getting myself in a situation, where I have to go to my acting class, or where I have to do a show in a comedy club with 300 people staring at me—just by doing that and getting through it and surprising myself with things that I feel are successful, I push myself back up into having confidence. I tell myself that I can have the freedom to fail, and I have the freedom to have a bad day and still get out there and do it. Because once I get through it and I turn around and look back at what I did, I'm really proud of myself."

She suggests picking goals that are actually attainable, instead of being futuristic. She also recommends Keith Johnston's "Impro" as inspiring reading. "I think it's really important to read a lot. It's so important as an actor to know about other people and other situations in other countries and other trends." She mentions that if an actor is young and out of work, it might be appropriate to think about graduate school, or working in another city. "Don't be afraid to take big chances, like hey, maybe I'll see what Florida's like, or Atlanta, or Chicago. I think people come to New York and get so caught up in the rat race, whether it's about the money or thinking, 'I know it's right around the corner and if I leave New York I'll lose it.' I just think that's ridiculous."

Mitchell Whitfield
Theatre: *"Brighton Beach Memoirs," "Biloxi Blues," "Ad Hock."* Film:
"Reversal of Fortune." TV: *"Monsters."* Voiceovers: *Macy's, Coke,
Pepsi, Milton Bradley.*

Mitchell Whitfield grew up in New York City, landing his first
professional job at 13. He has always supplemented his income
with voiceover work.

When Mitchell is out of work, he says he is very happy
staying at home, renting movies, eating Chinese food and playing video games. "I've become a vidiot. That is what keeps me
going during the dry spells." But, he adds, the most important
thing that helps him is an adjustment in his mental state, and
an ability to be relaxed. "Now that I know the business, I've
come to certain conclusions. One of them is that I get my share
of work, and not to worry if it's been a couple of weeks, or
three weeks or a month and I haven't booked something, because next month I could book eight or nine jobs in a one-
week period." For Mitchell it's a matter of understanding the
nature of the business, and not letting the pits and valleys
throw him. "The dry spots are the norm, they're not the exception, and it's nothing to worry about. Realizing that it's
nothing to worry about is half the battle."

Mitchell describes the trap of making every audition too
important. When things are slow, there is a tendency to put
all one's hope on that particular audition. He stresses the need
to forget about auditions after you complete them. Well, to try
to anyway: "It's going to get frustrating. The only thing you
can do is know that this is the way that it is, and things are
only going to get better from here." He talks about those times
when success has been dangled in front of him, when he came
close to something, when it's been between him and one other
person, or when casting people praise his talents and then give

someone else the job. His only recourse is to believe that "good people are going to work, whether it's right now or a few years from now. If you're good, you will eventually work. Part of that is having a strong sense of yourself and a strong sense of what you do. That doesn't mean banging on people's doors. It's just knowing, without even having to say it to anybody, 'I know what I can do and I will do it eventually.' "

For inspiration, he likes to think of actors like Robert Prosky, Wilford Brimley, or Brian Dennehy, actors who have made it in their later years. "So at the very worst you could say, 'Things could be bad for 15 years. When I'm 40 . . . ' " Mitchell emphasizes the need to stick it out and see how the game is played. "And it's not just knowing how to play the game," he adds, "but learning how to do what you want to do within it, and realizing that all the craziness, all the bad times are the norm. Things have gotten out of proportion in this business, out of balance. There are too many actors and too few jobs. It makes you feel powerless." But with all that in mind, it's still vital to go into an audition with self-confidence, and to maintain the ability to have a good time while doing it.

He comments that part of an actor's problem is that he is his own business, his own commodity, his own boss, his own employee. "When you look at a regular business, if something is going wrong, you can look at the product or the packaging and figure out what to do. But in this case, you have to look in the mirror, that's all you have. This puts a tremendous pressure on you and a lot of expectation. It's hard not to let the business affect you because it's your self. But this goes for the good parts, too. When someone tells how wonderful you are, let that be your reinforcement."

Jim Fyfe
Theatre: *"Artist Descending a Staircase," "Legs Diamond," "Biloxi Blues," "Privates on Parade," "Moonchildren."* TV: *"Encyclopedia Brown," "Tanner '88," "Dr. Fad Show."*

Jim Fyfe has been working professionally in New York City since 1983. He has worked as a temp or a caterer to support himself in the interim periods, and to satisfy his creative needs, he has done stand-up comedy and improv, and his own solo show, "A Normal Guy."

Jim attritubes part of his success to being a white, male actor. "That meant that the odds were on my side, which is just true, as any non-white, non-male will tell you." He admits that he's been very lucky, as most of his acting crises have been internal. Because he's been able to work, his disappointments come when he is dissatisfied with the quality of his own work, with the way something has been received, or watching a play he's in that he feels is being misdirected or misinterpreted. "When you expect something to launch your career and then it doesn't there is this huge disappointment, and things don't match up to your expectations a lot."

He emphasizes that one has to feel joy in what he is doing. If one is not enjoying the work, not spreading that good feeling to fellow actors or to the audience, Jim sees it as a natural course to wonder why one is doing it in the first place. "Because there are easier ways to make money and there are easier ways to get attention or love or approval. What comes up for me is, is this all just vanity?" During those times of frustration, Jim thinks it's extremely important not to place the blame outside of oneself, and to try to see each disappointment as a blessing in disguise. "You know the story about the boy digging through the pile of manure saying, 'There's gotta be a pony in here somewhere'? There's always a pony, there really is. You may not see it all the time, but the more willing you are to see it—which takes true humility, which I think finally is the key to great acting—the more you see that this is an opportunity for you to grow in some way, that this is in front of you for a reason."

When out of work, Jim suggests, "Just stop and lay back and take a look at what it is that you value and why you're doing this." He uses his time out to do rewrites on, and performances of, his one-man show. He plays his guitar, and performs stand-up comedy at local clubs. "I'm in charge of my creative satisfaction. That's my business, I can't expect anybody to give that to me." If an actor hits times of self-doubt, Jim believes it's crucial to understand that none of it is forever. "Art is not about this hermetically sealed world. That's a problem that a lot of actors have, that you get sealed into this world and you forget that theatre is the *mirror* unto reality; it is not the reality."

Jim points out that acting is a very demanding profession and while there are great gifts awaiting those who work hard and with the right spirit, there are also tremendous obstacles that are going to get in the way. He says reading "Creative Visualization," by Shakti Gawain, at the closing of "Legs Diamond" was being "immediately helpful in letting go of the anguish that I was embracing. I realized that a lot of what we identify as 'pain' is us saying, 'Oh god, it's pain.' Well, if you say 'Yes, that's pain,' like you say, 'That's blue,' then you're not trying to make it *not* pain. What happens a lot of times is that you embrace all your feelings of negativity. There's what is, and then there's the value we assign to what is. When the Dalai Lama won the Nobel Peace Prize and they asked him, 'How do you feel?' he said, 'Well, happy, but it's best not to get too excited one way or another about life.'"

* * * * * * * * *

If you're auditioning every day, there's a good chance that you're facing rejection every day. Even if you get one out of every ten jobs you audition for, that's still nine rejections to deal with. You always hear about persistence paying off, but the real key for each actor is in having a technology for going on when he or she feels like stopping.

First, actors point to the question of self-worth. If an actor puts his self-worth in a job, and doesn't get that job, then he starts to doubt himself. Many try not to identify at all with what they are doing, as the job is not about the person, but about the person's abilities. An actor performs the ability, is the storehouse for it, but he is not it. Everyone likes to get applause and recognition of hard work, but that can't be where the self-confidence is lodged. So if someone rejects a person's talent, for whatever reason, it's got nothing to do with the actor as a person.

In addition to keeping work separate, actors also say it's vital to have a safe home to return to. After an audition, one needs a clean, quiet place to go, to regroup. Then a person can take the time to remind himself who he is, what he believes in, what his priorities are, and why he is in this business in the first place. Actors usually come around to the fact that this is what they do best, and it's what they love doing more than anything else.

But let's say that a whole week goes into auditioning for something, and for one reason or another, the actor doesn't get the job. Many say they have to take all that frustrated creative energy and do something with it. It helps to throw oneself into another project right away. And it could be anything from writing a play to producing a solo show. If an actor is out there doing it, he's doing it, whether it's for money or not, no matter where the theatre is. That energy is used to propel oneself onward, instead of spiraling downward into depression.

All actors recommend having a good laugh as often as possible, doing personal researches, taking on work that has nothing to do with acting, and just being a student of human life. And all agree it is vital to remember that what actors do are "plays," and if it's not fun for them anymore, then it has ceased to be a "play."

* * * * * * * * * *

Since that article appeared, some updates are in order. Gabrielle Carteris went on to co-star in the Fox Network series, "Beverly Hills 90210." She recently signed for a second season. Mitchell Whitfield finished filming two more major movies: For Warner Bros., "Dog Fight" with River Phoenix and for Twentieth Century Fox, "My Cousin Vinny" in which he co-stars with Ralph Macchio and Joe Pesci.

14
From the Horse's Mouth......

The voice-over business is very much a people business, and some of the people you are about to meet help create the process. In doing these interviews, I've tried to ask questions that you not only would want answered, but also questions that would give you insight into the *people* and the *process*.

As you read this chapter you will find some contradictions among the answers. Just remember, opinions will vary. Not every agent, actor, or casting person thinks the same way.

Linda Weaver, Talent Agent

Linda Weaver is a voice-over talent agent at J. Michael Bloom, Ltd., in New York City. First, a little background. Linda grew up on an apple orchard in upstate New York. That certainly fits one of the criteria for being a talent agent. She got involved in medical genetic research at SUNY Purchase after a two-year stint at Vassar. She went on to work at Albert Einstein College of Medicine and then for a few years at Mt. Sinai.

For a short time after that, she was an unemployed actress doing soap-opera extra work. It was during that time that she decided to pursue the business of voice-overs and acting. She fell into being an assistant casting agent in voice-overs. From there, she moved up and on to become one of the most respected voice-over agents in the business.

We have just entered the nineties. What sound is hot ?

Linda: It's more contemporary, young thirties sort of damaged sound. It sounds like someone has been drinking and smoking too much. A whiskey voice. That's what's popular right now. I think it allows for new people to be brought into the business and I feel that the sound will remain popular for a very long time. It's interesting. It's different from anything we've heard in many years. You've got this voice that hits you. It grabs you.

When Martin Sheen did "Pepsi, The Voice of a New Generation," everybody said, "Wow, who is that?" Actually, the film "Apocalypse Now" started it. That was the first time people began to figure out that actors could do voice-overs. Most of the film narration in "Apocalypse Now" was done by Sheen. I believe it started the whole trend.

Also, there has been a shift in marketing trends. The target markets now are the "yuppies." And they, like the voices they listen to, are in their thirties. Also, they have more disposable income. So, it stands to reason that advertising is targeted to them.

Over the last five or six years, there has been a trend toward stage and screen actors doing voice-overs. I think in some cases it's good. Certain actors can translate and know how to use the technique. But a lot of them, unfortunately, cannot.

How big a part does credibility play?

Linda: A voice must, on a subliminal or subconscious level, be one that has appeal. It should instill trust. Consumers today are a lot more educated than they were years ago. And with dollars being tighter and things costing so much more, nobody willingly spends money on a product that they feel isn't going to yield results.

I really believe part of Martin Sheen's success is the fact that you do recognize him on some level. You might not be able to say, "That's Martin Sheen," but you know you've heard that voice before. And on a subliminal level, it instills a feeling of trust.

Linda, from the time that phone rings, how does the process work?

Linda: Basically, what happens is that a casting person with whom I have a relationship will call me and give me what is called a breakdown.

He gives me the conflict area [that is required by law], whether or not there is money available [anything over scale], and how the spot will run at the time of audition. Also at the time of audition, whether or not they require what is called a "clean contract." Let me explain: When casting directors request a clean contract, they are asking for all rights (foreign, theatrical, industrial, simulcast) at scale. This means a performer cannot strike off these provisions on the back of the SAG contract and that the performer waives the rights to negotiate these broadcast areas. The term "clean" refers to unstruck provisions.

The agent wants the performer to have the right to check off those provisions so that each category can be separately negotiated between client and agent. Even as we speak, the union has this clean contract issue on the table.

Assuming all this has taken place, the casting person describes to me the age of the voice and the timbre of the voice. I may even ask the casting person if he could choose anyone in the world for this commercial who would he choose? If he tells me, then I can get a prototype and this helps me. I then suggest names to him. He gets to select whom he wants to see.

The time slots vary. If he wants to see four actors, I'll get four time slots. A lot of actors think I have power over the number of people sent or time slots given. I don't often get the chance to say, "You must see this person because he's right." I may say it, but the casting person has the final approval.

Sometimes an actor will look to change agents because he thinks that another agent will be able to get him more time slots. The business simply doesn't work that way. Quite frankly, the agent who has the best rapport and the best relationship with the casting person, will indeed get the best time slots.

What are the best time slots?

Linda: The most times are best times. And the best time, I think, is the first day of casting. The second or third day usually means the casting person is worn out. I always prefer getting in the first day, if I can.

What criteria do you use when considering signing a voice-over person?

Linda: There are several different types of signs. One is a person who is very well established that you hope you can lure from another agency. And that, quite frankly, is dollars and cents. Nobody's kidding anybody about that. The other type of sign is a person you want to develop to fill in those empty spaces. And when you're looking at that, you take a look at your list and what the market demands. And you say, "Okay, most of the demands are in the age 30 with the interesting gritty voices. I've only got two signed clients in that category. I can probably use three or four more." So, if someone has that vocal quality that I hear from their tape, I may very well call them in for a talk.

Also, when I listen to a tape, I listen beneath what the product is. I try to listen to what they are doing with their sound. What kind of variety do they have? Where could I push this person vocally? How could I widen them?

By the way, I listen to every single tape that comes into the office, absolutely every tape, because you never know where you find new talent and I have found new talent, although I'd say it's only 1 percent of everything I've listened to, but by listening to tapes I have found people who are now making huge sums of money. It's taken two, three, five years, whatever it takes to get them to that point. But, yes, absolutely, I think it's important to find new talent that way.

Just as important is tapping into our agency's theatrical department to see who they meet. I try to find out who's an established actor or not so established, someone who may be somebody to groom towards voice-overs.

What factors go into the decision not to sign a performer?

Linda: When we decide not to represent someone, that doesn't mean he is not talented or will never work doing voice-overs. Sometimes it means we just cannot accommodate that style of voice. Very often a performer will be a little inexperienced and need some seasoning before signing with a highly competitive agency. It has happened that in the past we have not signed someone and several years later decided that the time was now right.

When you get a tape, do you listen to the whole thing?

Linda: Not always. If the tape is really, really bad, I may fast-forward and only listen to portions of it. But if a tape interests me, I'll listen two or three times before I decide whether or not to call somebody in. And, I always either write someone a note or call them, whether I like their tape or not, because I feel that if actors have taken all that time, money, and energy to put a tape together, they deserve a response.

Are you ever—how shall I say this—less than kind to someone sending you their tape?

Linda: Sometimes you have to be unkind, I guess. If you're telling somebody something they don't want to hear, you're unkind.

Besides listening to tapes, how else do you find new people?

Linda: There are several different ways. One is going to the theatre and finding out whether someone is represented. If they have an interesting voice they may or may not be interested in doing voice-overs. And by the way, a lot of people are still not interested, thinking it's the commercial thing with which they should not be associated. The other way is by chance, by hearing somebody in a restaurant, on the street, or wherever. Occasionally, more often than not, it's a woman's squeaky little voice that I can't make a lot of use of. But I sit and think, "It's a wonderful voice. That voice should be doing voice-overs."

Some casting people refer young actors to me. Our relationship is good enough so that they'll call me and say, "Listen, I think this guy's going to be hot. You should meet him." I do. And we've signed a number of people that way.

By the way, about going to shows? At this point, I limit

myself to Broadway and Off-Broadway. But it is our policy that our assistants go to showcases and find new talent. We actually increased the foreign language list by going to any number of Hispanic theatres, Japanese, and French productions. Our assistants are encouraged to participate, as a group, in bringing in new talent. That's in an effort to help them train to become agents. They interview, they learn how to deal with people, and they help decide whether or not we represent the talent.

I'm looking around the entire voice-over department and I see six desks spread over one large room. There are no partitions. What's the reason for that?

Linda: Yes. It's sort of like theatre in the round. It's useful because, for example, if I have an urgent call out to one of my voice-over talents, let's say the talent calls in and gets one of the other voice agents. I can hear that she is calling and intercept the call.

It also helps to be in this configuration when we get what is known as "casting block." And it happens to every single agent. I get a breakdown from a client. I hang up. Then I sit there and say, "I don't know who's right for this. Help!" I sort of throw it out to the other agents. Then, before you know it, suggestions fly and the juices flow again. The assistants participate in this. That's part of their learning process. They need to learn the voices. They need to develop their ear.

What is the best way for new people to contact you?

Linda: The best way is through referral, although that's not going to guarantee anything. It will guarantee that we'll listen to the tape. However, that would happen anyway at this agency. I've had people call me. They just get my name from someone and ask me how to break into voice-overs. I will usually tell them to record something on a tape recorder at home before they spend any money. I'll listen and evaluate it and tell them if it's worth anything. They can still do whatever they want. It is a subjective business, obviously, and my opinion is just that, my opinion.

But definitely sending you a reel is good?

Linda: It's like a resume. If you're looking for a job, you need to send out a resume. Your reel is your resume. And it should have a cover letter. I'm not talking about one of those cutesy cover letters meant to grab the attention. We are business people. It should be straightforward. Explain what your needs are and what your experience is. Tell me if you will call me on such and such a date or if I should call you. It's a business. It's not some little show that anyone is putting on. The cutesy stuff won't get my attention. A good letter and a good tape will get my attention.

Why do most talent agents freelance on-camera people and insist on signing voice-over people?

Linda: I think that the on-camera market, at least over the last three to five years, has demanded a lot more new people, so you need a constant influx of talent. Because of this, I don't know that an agent can service everybody properly by having them all signed. Also, an agent might free-lance on-camera people because there is not as much of an investment of time. But, I think it's essential to sign a voice-over because of the long-term career investment we make. The exception might be foreign language voices. We free-lance foreign language people because, although there is a demand, it's not enough to warrant signing anyone.

Because the voice is a lot less identifiable, it takes longer to establish. It takes us longer to build up someone's voice-over career. They are not going to book jobs so quickly. It usually takes the average signed client one to two years to start getting the work. But once they do, clearly, there is more longevity doing voice-overs.

Scott S. Linder, Talent Agent

Scott S. Linder graduated from Rutgers University with a degree in political science. He began working as an administrator on the college level. Later on, he decided to work in the entertainment industry. Since he wanted to learn about it from the bottom up, he moved right into the mailroom of one of the world's largest talent agencies. From there, it was on to another agency as an assistant. And now, for the past 15 years, Scott has been with Don Buchwald & Associates, where he is in charge of the voice-over department.

What is the basic difference between an assistant and a full agent?

Scott: An assistant is someone who has received a great deal of on-the-job training during an extended period of time while assisting a senior agent. The agent is a professional who is hired by performers to find them job opportunities and then negotiate their fees. You are trained to be aware of the various employment rates as dictated by the actor's unions. And, of course, there are decisions you can't learn from a manual. Should your client endorse a particular product? Is the money being offered sufficient? Is this a wise career choice?

The agent should be sensitive to the professional needs of his client. However, the agent must also be aware of his client's emotional needs. Performers require considerable caring and reassuring. The agent, as the middleman, bears the brunt of much frustration from both the actor and the casting director. Both individuals want something. Sometimes it is a perfect match. But, usually, a lot of negotiating is required.

We have an interdependent relationship with our buyers (casting directors and agencies). In the commercial talent business, we deal with so many casting calls on a daily basis that any agent who can succeed in this area can very easily transfer his agenting skills to any other part of the entertainment industry. There is a clear distinction between casting director and agent: The casting director seeks out specific talent for a particular job: an on-camera commercial, a radio commercial, a television voice-over. It is the function of the agent to supply the appropriate actors and/or announcers.

Scott, what do you look for when you sign new people?

Scott: Because of our "exclusive" relationship with our clients, we only add to our list performers who will supplement it—celebrities who are always being sought after and voices that are currently considered in vogue by the creative advertising community.

Our research has revealed that the advertisers are currently seeking the "thirtysomething" types to promote cars, food products, even major corporations. You no longer need the deep, resonant, mellifluous voice to be "the voice of . . . ." The industry is now using more women and celebrities for their needs. However, I strongly believe that there will never be a replacement for the rich, romantic, wonderful announcer used in the past.

Scott, in the business you are known as a tough agent. How do you respond?

Scott: As I said earlier, the agent is the middleman who must walk the tightrope of decision-making. You can be blamed or praised by either side. I care very much about the performers we are privileged to represent. These are people who have been in the business from 40 years down to beginners. Each has different needs. But I feel a major responsibility to them and indirectly, to their families.

It is my job to get them as many employment opportunities and have them earn as much money as possible. I work very hard to accomplish this, and my aggressive means may be perceived as "tough" by casting directors and agency people. I take this as a compliment. I also know that I am fair. I feel it's a perfect combination for being a successful agent.

Let's say two years from now, the vogue voice goes out of fashion. Do you drop that client?

Scott: No. Hopefully, that client is also an actor who would probably transcend that fad period and be just as capable working in many other areas in the voice-over and radio field.

Here's that same tired line, "Everyone thinks they can do voice-overs." How do you respond?

Scott: You can be an established performer, an actor who has starred in major films and on the Broadway stage. But, in front of the microphone, you may not have the right technique in order to interpret or sell the writer's copy. I don't care how great an actor you are—unless the advertiser wants you because of who you are, you are not going to win the job.

It's important that an agent knows his client's talents and limitations. That comes from seeing the actor perform on the stage, attending recording sessions, and auditioning the actor up at the agent's office.

We have to use the actor's talents as broadly as possible in order to make sure no one in the casting world stereotypes or pigeonholes the talent's abilities. The more an actor can do, hopefully, the more money he can make.

Jeffrey D. Howell, Talent Agent

Jeffrey D. Howell is the director of the voice-over department at Abrams-Rubaloff & Lawrence in Los Angeles, California.

Jeff was born in Roanoke, Virginia, and spent his teen-age years working in over 50 community theatre productions. His interests led him to Boston University where he graduated from the College of Communications with a bachelor's degree in broadcasting and film and a minor in marketing. While in Boston, Jeff worked at a local radio and television station and at a theatrical public relations agency.

Upon arriving in Los Angeles, he became employed as an extra casting director and cast numerous television and film projects. During this period, Jeff realized that he was interested in working more closely with actors. After considerable research, he landed an assistant's position at Abrams-Rubaloff & Lawrence (ARL). He attributes his success at ARL to his background in a variety of related fields.

Jeff, in New York, an actor can free-lance in the voice-over field. Is it true that in California a voice-over person must have an agent?

Jeff: Yes. I think that is definitely true. This is mainly because, in Los Angeles, the voice-over auditions are mostly held at the agent's office. Ad agencies call us directly. We actually record the talent in our recording booth and send it back to the agency where they select who they want. So you see, if you don't have an agent, you don't have access to the call.

How much voice-over casting is done in the agent's office?

Jeff: About 90 percent. A free-lance actor could send his demo tape directly to a casting company. However, if the actor doesn't have an agent pushing him, trying to get him in, the casting company may not see you. There are a limited number, of audition times, so the casting people would rather audition actors they know or ones the agents recommend.

Is there more voice work now in Los Angeles?

Jeff: Yes. Recently, more commercial production has moved to Los Angeles from New York and so, too, have a lot of actors. This is based on my conversations with industry sources in New York.

What do you look for when you're looking to sign a new sound?

Jeff: Well, I hate to say "different" and "unique," because you hear that all the time. However, I think it's true that while looking for the next voice of " ?, " and I think we're all looking for that, I also look for a voice with flexibility, with talent. That's hard to come by. When I receive demo tapes, I listen to them and I try to hear what's going on underneath the voice, not just the voice itself. That's something people don't understand. They have to be able to act, to analyze the copy, and know what's happening in the spot. They can't just get behind the microphone and read. Unfortunately, with many people, that's what happens.

I know that one of your next questions is going to be, "How do we make those decisions?" Well, there are several different ways in which I get talent. First of all, I get calls from talent who may not be happy with their current representation. If the talent is heard on a lot of spots in the Los Angeles market, or nationally, we are obviously more interested in meeting with the talent. However, there are no guarantees.

We also find actors through referrals, through other actors or agency people. And finally, I listen to demo tapes, every last one of them. I take notes so that when I call them or they call me, I can, at least, give some feedback.

And if we invite actors to audition, it doesn't mean they are going to be signed automatically. We evaluate their talent through a rigorous audition process. We want to make sure that demo tape wasn't just a glossy representation.

Demo tapes can be so deceiving. You can spend hours in a booth, put a lot of production under the voice, and with some decent copy, you can actually get something that sounds pretty good. This explains why we audition people in-house and try to strip that away and really get down to the basics. We give them several different types of copy, including some character copy, just to see what they can do. Plus, we give them direction so that we can see how well they take it.

Where else do you find new clients?

Jeff: Theatre. Most of the time I go because one of our actors is appearing. During or after the performance, I'll whip out my pen and make notes on my program. After a performance, I often approach an actor with whom I was impressed and ask if he or she is represented. After attending a film, I'll try to remember the credits. Then I'll run to my car and write down the names. The next day I'll call SAG or AFTRA and find out if the actor has commercial representation.

I don't think actors looking to get into commercials truly understand how competitive voice-over is. And I'll tell you why: because some actors don't realize that many of the voice people have been in the business for years. Their voices do not age as quickly as their appearance. It's not a visual medium. And the longer these actors are around, the more they are known. In some cases, producers call and ask for the talent by name. They've obviously had a prior working relationship with the actor.

So the new actor has to understand the competitiveness of

this business and how difficult it can be to, not only get in, but also to survive in it as well. There are actors who have already established a reputation in this business. When they were first starting, it used to be that they could go to 15 voice-over auditions and book one. Now, for the new crop of performers, it could be up to about 50-plus to one.

I have a few actors in my department who have not quite hit their stride. Some have gone a year without catching on. It's my responsibility to push their voices to the ad agencies and to the casting companies. Once the actors land one, hopefully others will follow. Sometimes it's only a matter of getting that first one. Sometimes it's not. Maybe it will take 10. Actors need to understand that. In Los Angeles, the competition is fierce. There are only a dozen or so talent agencies that represent the actors for voice-over. And they have just so many voice categories to fill. Most of us do not want to get too talent-heavy. We want to represent all of our talent effectively. So, you can see how tight it can get.

How many voice-over people are signed with your agency?

Jeff: I would say about 175. That's just voice.

How does that 175 break down?

Jeff: Of that group, probably 75 percent are men. As we all know, and though we may not like it, men work more in the voice-over business than do women. However, that is changing, albeit not fast enough. However, we're now hearing women's voices on car commercials. I'm hoping there's much more to follow.

As far as the age range among those 175, for the men and women, it spans between 25 and 60-plus. However, clients are buying the baby boomers, ages 30-45. So that's what I must have a good supply of. Of course, when I speak of age, I mean how old they sound.

Not too long ago, it was the 25 to 30 sound. What happened?

Jeff: I would say that the late 20s is certainly popular. But still the 30s to 40s range is what's being bought. That includes the young fathers. We're hearing a lot of dads on spots, as well as character actors, especially in comedy spots. It's not so much the young stand-up comedian, the way it was last year. This year the trend is actors that have a comedy background.

A point I feel needs covering: Actors must market themselves. I get calls from actors who want representation and I can't represent them. They ask, "Well then, how can I get more exposure in this market, so that I am attractive to a talent agency?" I tell them that if they have a good enough demo reel—a higher quality demo reel—they could send it to corporations, big businesses, and companies with audio visual departments that may do their own casting.

The actor should think about who is buying voices out there, other than the ad agencies. There are animation houses. And sometimes, believe it or not, they will be open to hearing voices that have been submitted directly to them. These are some ways that the actors can market themselves.

Here's a point: The voice-over actor should realize how important it is to constantly train. There are things they can do at home, or in their cars, to help them stay in shape. For example, they can choose a tongue twister or a vowel sound pattern that they can say aloud on the way to auditions. Their mouths—not only their brains—have to be warmed up. They have to be able to form the words.

A lot of times our clients come up here to audition. They are in a rush. Other things are going on in their lives. They get into the booth and even though they've said, "I read it over," unfortunately, it's not coming out. And that's because their mouths and their tongues aren't warmed up. And sometimes even their vocal chords aren't warmed up. Look, a body builder trains. So why wouldn't a voice-over actor?

Also, if actors are interested in doing cartoons, they should watch cartoons. They need to know what's going on in the market. I tell my commercial actors that they should be listening to the radio and the television to hear what's happening out there. I may say, "I need the voice of so-and-so cola." They may not have seen or heard that spot. The actors must educate themselves.

Les Perkins, Creative Director for
Disney Character Voices, Domestic

Les was instrumental in establishing this new division of The Walt Disney Company in 1988. Les and his staff supervise the casting, scripting, and direction of existing Disney characters as they are recorded throughout all divisions of the corporation.

Les has been with The Walt Disney Company for over 14 years in a variety of creative areas, including Walt Disney Imagineering and Educational Productions where he worked as a writer and producer. In addition to his current position, he has been a casting and recording director and production manager of animated series and specials for network television. Les has done his share of performing, too—as the voice of "The Mad Hatter," "Caterpillar," and "Mr. Toad."

How do you get to know about the new voices?

Les: It's really a combination of two things . . . We review actors' previous auditions for us. Although they may not be right for that part, we remember them for future projects. The other way is through demo tapes. We do listen to demo tapes—that question gets asked a lot. As a matter of fact, one of the actors I know is always amazed because I hired him from a demo tape that I received four years before! I had listened to the tape, liked the voice, it wasn't right for anything I needed then, but I remembered it was a good voice. So when a part finally came up I called him in.

By necessity, we have to rely heavily on finding talent through the voice-over agents. Gone are my early days of casting when I could spend time helping newcomers. I felt it was important to give back or to help out new talent because I too was just starting out, and people had given me a break. I would try to give as much time as I could to encourage new talent or to find new people. I still do, but not as often. Unfortunately, what happens to all casting people is you finally get so busy and have so many things to accomplish in one day that you lose the time to be personable. And where I used to be able to spend time on the phone with people, I no longer can. So what I recommend voice actors do is send a nice cover letter—maybe a follow-up postcard—along with their demo tape. You just have to trust that casting directors will listen to it. It's annoying for me to get a phone call saying, "I hope you got my demo tape. Did you listen to it?" We just don't have time to respond to people that way. And then there's always the story—and this is true, it's one of the peculiarities of the business—where somebody does a follow-up phone call, or just happens to call somebody cold, and the timing is right and boom, they get the audition or they get the part. That kind of stuff does happen. It's a difficult tightrope for actors to walk—when are they promoting themselves appropriately and when are they being too pushy?

We get many calls from people wanting to audition for us.

To accommodate those calls we've installed a separate phone line with a prerecorded message that spells out what the newcomer needs to know. For the benefit of the readers of this book, here's the announcement: "Hello, and welcome to the Disney Character Voices information line. If you are interested in getting into the voice-over business, following are some suggestions that may be helpful.

First of all, voice-over work is not simply making funny voices; it's acting. If you lack acting experience, we strongly suggest enrolling in a voice-over workshop. Various workshops are advertised in publications, such as *Drama-Logue*, *Variety*, and other trade papers. Local colleges or universities may offer similar courses. Good classes will not only enhance your acting abilities, but also teach you about microphone techniques, proper voice placement, developing new character voices, and provide general facts about the voice-over industry that will be of value to your future success.

When you're ready to present your talents, the next step is to make a demonstration tape. Professional tapes are approximately three minutes in length and exemplify a variety of voices and acting styles. They may feature both character and narrative voices. Your demo tape serves as your calling card to agencies as well as producers.

If you currently do not have an agent, we suggest submitting your completed demo tape to talent agencies. Nearly all voice casting at The Walt Disney Studios is done through agent representation. There are many voice-over agencies in Los Angeles, New York, and Chicago; these are listed with the Screen Actors Guild and the American Federation of Television and Radio Artists. It is then the agencies' responsibility to make casting directors and producers aware of your talents by sending them a copy of your demo tape, arranging for auditions, and recommending your talents when appropriate projects come up.

In review, we suggest: 1. Enroll in a voice-over workshop. 2. Make a demonstration tape; and 3. Find agent representation.

If you are calling from out-of-state, here is some additional information. Most voice-over work is done in Los Angeles, New York, or Chicago. We rarely look outside these areas for new talent, as these cities are plentiful with very gifted actors and actresses. Voice work is done on a free-lance basis, and long-term contracts are rare. Your local radio, TV, or advertising agencies are a good place to start and may help you get the experience you'll need to compete in the larger cities.

Finally, we wish you success in your endeavors and hope this message has been both helpful and informative. You may send us your demo tape if you'd like; however, please do not call us for a response or for comments regarding your tape. We will contact you or your agent only if and when there is an appropriate audition. You may send your tape to:

Disney Character Voices, Inc.
350 S. Buena Vista Street
Burbank, CA 91521

Thank you for your interest in The Walt Disney Company and in Disney Character Voices!"

When you do get demo reels, are they reels of commercials or cartoons?

Les: I get them both and I need both. I need to be able to hear their natural voice—where an actor is coming from. This is a favorite story of mine. I auditioned a lady once because her voice tape began, "Hi, this is [her name]." The rest of her tape was a lot of different commercials. There wasn't a single voice that was right on the rest of her tape. But her natural voice, her "Hi, this is . . . ," those words had the right potential I was looking for and I called her in for an audition. She didn't get that job, but I have since hired her for other things. So I always say, I want to hear the natural voice, even on a cartoon reel. The other reason I need to hear their commerical reel is because I want to hear their acting ability. You can't always hear acting ability as well on standard cartoon work. You can get a better sense of it on a commercial reel.

In casting for features, Disney looks for a very natural style. We don't want people who do interesting voices, we want people who have interesting voices naturally. Then we can build the personality out of that voice. For example, take a veteran Disney voice like Sterling Holloway, whose outstanding performances include the Cheshire Cat from "Alice in Wonderland," Kaa, the snake from "The Jungle Book," and "Winnie The Pooh." They're all pretty much the same voice print. But you don't think of Kaa while watching Pooh. He created distinct peronalities through his acting. A lot of that also has to do with the quality of the writing. Television work is different.

Some advice for people who are interested in doing voices for animated films.

Les: For openers, I can't stress enough the importance of acting, especially in cartoon work. Cartoon work is not a series of funny voices and funny noises. It's exaggerated acting, and often, it's creating a personality and character with an unusual or distinctive sound. But the acting ability is the most important. All the emotions have to be conveyed vocally. I encourage everybody to take voice-over workshops and other acting classes. I always hesitate suggesting something to people just starting out that's going to cost them money, but on the other hand, they're entering a very specialized field. You're only doing yourself a disservice if you enter into that arena without being prepared.

It's important to come across strong. First impressions are very lasting, and if you're not quite ready yet, people remember that you're an amateur and that will stay with you for a long time. It shouldn't be that way, but that's the way people are. So it's important to have a strong demo tape and to show variety in what you can do. And it isn't just a variety of voice styles and dialects. It's more important to be able to create personalities, so that somebody listening to the tape can get a visual image of what that character looks like and how it moves, because that's what the animators are going to go on.

For people who really want to get into cartoon work, taking an improv class is very helpful.

Why improv?

Les: So much of television cartoon work is comedy, the actor's ability to take a script that's written and be able to plus it [add to it]. In any work, a director looks to an actor to bring something to the copy—some extra life. Actors have got to be careful though. You don't want to start doing shtick or adding stuff just for the sake of doing it.

Frequently, actors are called on to think on their feet—to supply ad libs for the various characters they are doing. This is where having an improv background can be an invaluable asset.

Are there cartoon voice classes?

Les: Yes. There are a lot of classes here in Los Angeles. Some voice actors have workshops that primarily teach cartoons.

However, I'd like to add that I believe acting is an innate ability. You can expand or refine your repertoire, learn techniques for quicker access, but you can't learn talent. Either ya got it or ya don't. Some of our actors joke during recording sessions, when we ask for another take, "Once more with talent!"

What's a "sound-alike"?

Les: What we do is a bit unique in the industry. Our job here is to help carry on the integrity and consistency of the personalities and sounds of the established Disney characters. For instance, Jiminy Cricket, Goofy, Donald Duck. The people who originally created those voices are no longer around. But the characters still have a life in television shows, theme park shows, ice shows, home videos, educational productions, toys, records, computer games, even feature films. It's important that they sound the same. I mean, people have the film "Cinderella" in their homes, so kids know what the Fairy Godmother sounds like. To maintain the believability and appeal of that character in new uses, it's important that we maintain the consistency of that personality. Part of that is done through the voice print. The rest of it is accomplished through the writing and direction—what I call the "triad of personality." When we have a casting need, it's usually very specific. We want to match a particular sound. We create a reference tape of soundtrack material and send that to the agents. They usually audition people in their office. When we get the audition tapes from the agents, we listen and try to find the best matches to the original. Out of the average 50 submissions, we'll call in those half a dozen or so that are the closest in sound and audition them ourselves.

Out of all those people, you'd only call in six?

Les: We're lucky on most characters if we can get two people who are close. It's very difficult. I worked with one casting director in town who said to me, "This is the hardest assignment I've ever done. I don't envy you at all. What you do is so incredibly specialized." It's extremely difficult for the actor, because we're not asking for an impression. We're asking for an actor to take on somebody else's personality and understand the speaking rhythms, attitudes, and how that character thinks. It's an established character, so in a sense it's easier, because the actor has a reference model for what to do or can learn what to do. But it's also difficult because it's not their creation. They have to study the original performance and integrate it into their own personality and style and develop something that feels natural to them, yet is still consistent with our character. Then they have to *own* the character themselves. At first it's mechanical. The more the actor performs with consistent direction, the better he gets.

How do you find your sound-alikes?

Les: We know who's out there from years of experience. So we can come up with a basic list of potentials. I'll also sit down and go through the demo tapes and my casting notes. As we listen to demo tapes, we make notes on the box about anything that describes the voice so I can refer back to them. Then we ask the agents for their recommendations.

I have tremendous respect for what actors go through. I can't say enough to support them. At one point in my life, I was thinking about a performing career. Later, I decided to be on the production side, not the stage side. It's a crazy business and crazy pressure that actors are under, being in a constant free-lance environment, being judged on every-

thing they do. What I always tell new actors is that just because you didn't get the part doesn't mean you've failed. You
can't think like that. You go into an audition and your job is
to give a good audition. Whether or not you get the part—
I mean that's what you're there for. You can't totally dismiss
it—you have to have the mind set like, "It doesn't really matter. All I really want to do is perform well at the audition."
There are a lot of factors that go into hiring a person. You
can only hire one. That's the unfortunate thing. And just because you didn't get it doesn't mean you didn't do a good
job. There may have been five people who were equally as
good. Only one person gets it. And there are a lot of management or network decisions that play into this. The best
person doesn't always get the job. But if you gave a good
audition, the casting director should remember that.

Also, don't give up your day job until you're well established. This is a reality. Anyone should have some kind of
back-up. It's dangerous if you specialize too much. Voice-over
people can go in trends. Somebody who's very hot one year
can burn out through overexposure, and then suddenly it's
three or four years later and nobody's hiring him. His voice
has been over-used.

The voice-over community is a relatively small group, but
it has a community feel. A lot of the actors know each other,
and they're very supportive of each other's work. I've had
auditions where an actor says, "I'm not right for this part, but
so-and-so might be." I got floored the first time I heard an
actor suggest somebody else. But what goes around, comes
around. You can't help but respect and think nicely of that
actor."

Michael Mislove and Nellie Bellflower, Actors

Michael Mislove's career has come full circle. As a kid he used to sit in front of a tape recorder, an old Webcor, and pretend he was a radio announcer. Now his voice is heard on countless commercials. In college, when Michael realized the radio station only had eight watts, he shifted his focus to theatre, and, after college, ended up doing comedy. Michael put together "The Ace Trucking Company," an improv comedy group, doing many shots on the "Tonight Show," among other TV appearances. He wound up out in California. When the group split up, Michael went on to co-write and produce the film, "Tunnelvision." One of its stars was Nellie Bellflower. Nellie and Michael moved back east where their respective commercial careers took off. Today, Michael's voice beams across the country on a little more than just eight watts.

Nellie Bellflower went on her first audition early in her college days in California. At the audition she was asked if she could roller skate. Without missing a beat, she replied "yes," even though she had never skated in her life. She got the job. It was a television show.

Next, a casting person told her she had better leave Los Angeles and go do theatre in New York because she wasn't pretty enough to make it in Hollywood. I had better let you readers know now, Nellie is gorgeous. The blond-haired, blue-eyed gorgeous that I have always dreamed of being!

Nellie has gone on to play starring roles in many television shows like "Barney Miller," "Police Woman," and "Barnaby Jones." Nellie played Fonzie's girlfriend, The Lone Stripper, in "Happy Days." The list goes on. Today, she is heard on hundreds of radio spots and television voice-overs.

What should the new voice-over actor be aware of?

Michael: When you're first starting out in this business, it's hard to know the ropes. However, unless you do, unless you've been around the block a few times, you're going to get had. Like when I first started out, I found myself coming into an audition, picking up the copy, and one or two people would come over and engage you in conversation. And you, who are trying to get to know everybody, to be gracious, get into the conversation.

Suddenly, your name is called. MICHAEL MISLOVE, and you're next. You don't know enough to say, "Well, I haven't had a chance to read the copy." Now you're not sure that this person engaged you in conversation on purpose. But, you see, they've probably already been in and read. Then they say, "Bye, bye," and hit the elevator. You're tripping into the room and trying desperately to look over the copy on the way in. You get in and they say, "Okay, take one." You go, "Wha?" They say, "Thank you very much." You're out the door! Two weeks later, you see the same person again and suddenly they say, "Oh, how are you?" Same thing, another engaging conversation. By the way, never walk into an audition, pick up a piece of copy that has already been marked, and think, "Gee, this is great! I don't have to sit here and figure out the whole thing. I'll just go in with this." That's a no-no.

Nellie: Most people think that things are simplistic. For instance, if you are pretty, you should be an actress. If you are handsome, an actor. It's the same thing with voice-overs. People say, "You have such an interesting voice, you should do voice-overs." That's what people think commercials are all about. All you have to have is an interesting voice or be pretty and you can make it.

Michael: Lots of people think that you can sit at home, hear a commercial and say, "Gee, I can do that so much better. Everyone tells me I have such a great voice." It's kind of like sitting home and watching quiz shows and seeing those people answer all the questions. Sure, at home you answer the questions just perfectly. But get up in front of that camera, with those lights on, and the people staring at you . . . you go blank. You can't remember your name. You're off the show. You won a box of corn flakes and that's it. You're gone.

Everyone has a "nice voice." It doesn't matter. You have to have something special. And, you have to know what to do with it. Early in my career, while I was still with The Ace Trucking Company, I was about to go out to California. One member of the group said, "You know, you really should start doing commercials." I asked her what it entailed. She said, "You go on auditions and they give you jobs!" She didn't actually say that. But that's what I heard. I went up to my agent at the time and told him I wanted to do commercials.

He said, "Oh, you do, do you?"

"Yes, I do."

"When do you want to start doing them?" he asked.

"Immediately."

"Have you ever gone up on an audition for a commercial?"

"No, but it can't be any different from what I'm doing. And I want to do voice-overs, not on-camera. I hear it's good money and you don't have to work as hard."

"I'll tell you what," he said. "We're having a demo audition and a few people from the agencyy are coming in. I would like you to come in and read some copy."

I said, "Okay, if I have to try out." I was very young.

So, later that day, I went up to a studio and I walked in the door and there I saw E. G. Marshall, David Birney, Meredith Baxter [Birney], and Annie Hoffman [Dustin Hoffman's wife]. One at a time, they all read. And they were very good. The agent gave me this copy for some car and told me to go in and read it. It was right about there that I started to feel the first pangs of maybe I shouldn't be here.

Somehow I got through it. When it was over, my agent called me over. He played back the take and asked me what I thought. I said it sounded pretty good! He said, "It is. It's pretty good. It's not great. You have to work on this. This is not something you just walk in off the street and do. Great will get it. Pretty good won't."

People often say, "I think I'm great. How do I get started? How do I get heard?" What's your response?

Michael: Well, without knowing if the person has any talent, I will always couch everything in "if you're any good," you have to exhibit it. If it's voice-overs, you have to have something on tape that says, "You're good."

You just can't walk in any place and expect to be heard if you don't have the proper equipment, like a reasonably good voice-over tape. I don't mean something that looks like it's been festering under a rug, with a handwritten label, recorded in your kitchen. That's embarrassing. Take classes, study hard, and earn money doing anything else. Get a good tape made.

Then send it to EVERYBODY. Every agent. Every independent casting person. Every agency casting person. Every production company. You never know who will listen and who will call you. You have to get it out there.

Nellie: I have a real view on this—not so much how to get into commercials but on being an actor. If somebody wants to be a painter or a writer, he would not assume he could just paint a great picture or write the great novel. You can't do anything for which you haven't prepared.

A lot of this business has little to do with whether or not you have a good voice. A lot of it is the business of acting, the meeting of people. I think until you've gone out there, until you've gone to offices, until you've pounded on doors, until you've tried to get agents, until you've taken classes, until you've done everything that is part of the pain and part of the joy of being in this business, you can't even begin to try to make a living at it. It's an apprenticeship. Now, every once in a while, someone comes in and strikes it lucky. And because that happens, people think that's going to be them.

Michael, what are the toughest kinds of sessions?

Michael: I think they're demo sessions. There can be so much tension during a demo session. The reason could be that the creative team at the ad agency is really crazed: They are dealing with the client who probably told the creative team on this given day, that if the work was not good, "You guys are off. We're going to another agency." You, the talent, don't realize that these people are under that kind of pressure.

The sessions are tough. They are very exacting. Every word, every phrase must be stressed a certain way. Some of these sessions get so extreme, they're called "sessions from hell." I've seen wonderfully professional people reduced to angry masses or to tears. People who you would never in a million years think would lose it, do lose it at these sessions. Everything is taken so personally.

One of the nice things about our business is that a lot of the actors in voice-overs did not start out to be in voice-overs. Most are still actors, concentrating in theatre, film, television, and most of them are still doing that. They use the voice-over talent to supplement their income. Some of them enjoy doing voice-overs so much, and have done so well doing it, that they say, "Wait a minute, enough with the road, enough with going to Albany for three weeks with the play that may never open. I can make money doing this and enjoy my life." They've reached a point where they can do that.

And I've never experienced the level of support that almost everyone gives to each other. There doesn't seem to be that cut-throat mentality. Therefore, it becomes like a big club.

The auditions turn into kind of social events. That could drive a lot of casting directors nuts. While they're trying to audition people, everyone outside is having this party. "Hey, how are you? Haven't seen you in three days . . . ."

Nellie: Most friendships in show business last about as long as the project. They last as long as the movie you are making, the play that you're in. And you all promise that you're going to see each other and that you are going to be friends forever.

Sort of like sleep-away camp.

Nellie: Exactly. But in commercials, you have a continuing relationship over the years. It's the same people, the same immediacy in the relationships as in a play or a movie. "I want to know everything about you—and eat your entire face!" And then you see that person three days later, and three days later, and it keeps on that way. You build incredible bonds. If you think about it, commercials are like 30-second plays. You get to be a character. You get to do something creative. Sometimes you get the chance to think up something new and different.

And a television series, in my opinion, is just a very long commercial. Look who's doing them. Hollywood directors are directing commercials. Hollywood writers are writing commercials and filmmakers are filming commercials.

Marcia Savella, Actor

Marcia Savella's background is as diversified as her voice-over and on-camera capabilities. Born in Edgewood, Rhode Island, she began exhibition ballroom lessons at 7, ballet at 12, developed hips and boobs by 15, and so professional dancing took a back seat to her theatrical career. She worked in theatre throughout high school and got her Equity card before receiving her BFA from the University of Connecticut. Marcia has appeared extensively on Broadway, Off-Broadway, in regional and stock productions, as well as in various stints on television and in film.

She is most recognized for her work, both straight and character, as a commercial voice actress ranging from industrials, narrations, animation, cartoons, and dubbing to—you name it!

Do you think there was anything during your earlier years that might have helped prepare you for what you do today?

Marcia: Ironically, I think it might have been my first-grade teacher, Mrs. Lennon. It was the way that she taught us to read. She was extraordinary; she taught everything in phonetics. The longer the word, the more fun it was for me to see if I could pronounce it phonetically. I was able to break up the word. When you are taught that this is the way to read, there's nothing that you can't read. As time went on in school, one of the things I loved to do was cold read, which really helps you in this business.

Strangely enough, that desire to take a large word and get the fun out of pronouncing it correctly was perfect training for narration work, where all of a sudden you're faced with pages and pages of medical narration about strange diseases or technical automotive terminology and you can read through it almost without a hitch. When you can zip right along in the industrial field where you've got 50 pages of copy, not 60 seconds, it makes you an asset to the client.

A lot of being able to do this is making your eyes move quickly. I usually try to choose a pace, and my mind is going 50,000 times faster than the pace at which I am reading. It's almost like if I see a comma, my eyes have already gone two sentences ahead. I've fed into my brain what it's going to sound like, and then the entire script just begins to happen.

I have a certain theory. People who like to do games and puzzles really like to do voice-overs, because it's taking something basic and molding it into a shape and finding out what does and doesn't make it work.

I love to take a script, look at it, and the first thing I'll say is, "What do I think they want? What's the predictable read?" Then I always try to give one of my reads as a predictable one. Then I will find at least two other choices, hopefully ones that no one else chooses. Those are the unpredictable reads. And especially in an arena now, where you are auditioning against 30 or 40 other people, what's going to get you the job may not only be the best reading but a memorable one.

If you have an interpretation that nobody else has, it's frustrating if a casting person says, "Okay, fine, we're going to do just one take." Then you have to make a choice. Do you give the predictable read, which may be what they thought they were looking for? Or do you take a chance and go anti-type and give something that's interesting and different?

Marcia, you can imitate almost anything you hear! From where do you think that ability stems ?

Marcia: As a child, I had no formal training for dialects or character sounds. I was an only child and my Mom and Dad and I used to go off in the car on weekends. We would do a lot of singing in the car. My mother loved the "Wizard Of Oz," so she and I would do the entire score! We'd do the Wicked Witch, Toto, and all the Munchkins [upper-register ones and lower-register ones]. Actually the placement of my voice for the Munchkins became a very important placement for a lot of other characters. I call it the helium sound with a tremolo, sort of like an insecure soprano. You see, all those years we did that, I never thought of it as a skill. I thought everyone's family did this.

I spent a lot of solo play time that was probably creatively spent towards this business, although, at the time, I had no idea. I don't think anyone steps out and says, "Wow, when I grow up, I really want to do voice-overs." I would mimic records and people I saw on television. And because I was an only child, I tended to listen to and watch things that were more adult. For example, I spent lots of time watching the "Jack Paar Show." And some of the people who were really imitative favorites of mine were Hermione Gingold, Zsa Zsa Gabor, and Julie Andrews.

Now, Julie Andrews has a sort of slide. Her voice would kind of slide into everything. Once you get that slide you have the basic key to her. It's so important to get a quick handle on a dialect or an accent. If I want to cue into a British sound, I might think Sarah Miles: "Ryan's Daw'ta, Ryan's Daw'ta. . . ." The way she would say "daughter" would instantly kick me in.

Certain sounds will instantly kick in the dialect. Like German, the placement is in the front of the mouth with a somewhat tight jaw. French is puckered in the front but then it quickly sneaks some air around to the back of the throat for the guttural sounds. I'm sure that all this came from sitting around as a kid listening to things.

Now here's something that people may not put together. Knowing and understanding geography is an important asset when you're doing dialects.

To know what countries border on what other countries helps me. For example, certain things in French will take on a Spanish flair if they are in the Basque region.

It's similar for languages. You may look at a Spanish word and know what the pronunciation is because you have an innate knowledge of how the language sounds. Then you can create what the English sounding dialect is like. Not the Spanish pronunciation, but how someone who speaks Spanish would pronounce an English word, just because you have that working knowledge.

What would you admit to being one of your biggest frustrations in this business?

Marcia: It would have to be when a casting person forgets that it's a voice business, which should mean the talent has no age, no sex, no anything. If I hear an actress say to me, "Gee, I really wanted to go up for this role, but they wanted a teen-ager," and if I know that this woman, who may be in her 50s, does a terrific teenager because she has a light sound, it's frustrating that somebody wouldn't see her because she's not a teen-ager.

Fortunately there are some casting people who are open-minded enough to say, "Well, I don't care how young or old the actress is, I know she does this."

I have a wide range and love to try anything. I have been asked to do anything from babies to octogenarians. That only happens if a casting person realizes that they are not casting a film or a theatre piece. It is a *sound* production. The magic of the voice is what's important. Make no mistake, many casting people are wonderful about giving you the latitude to read anything. I applaud those people.

Another big frustration is dealing with a casting person either from an agency or an independent, who is young, inexperienced, and does not understand anything about the business or about acting, who's never done a script before, and who doesn't understand comedy or the law of threes. It's also unfair to them. How could they be expected to give meaningful direction or understand and speak the same language, if they've never been exposed to any of it?

For the benefit of those who do not know, what is the law of threes?

Marcia: Man One: So, what did you get from the store?
Man Two: I got shoes.
Now, that's not really funny.
Man One: So, what did you get?
Man Two: I got shoes and tomatoes.
Still not really funny.
Man One: So, what did you get?
Man Two: I got shoes, tomatoes, and a salami.
Now that's funny. You don't know why, but it sounds funnier when there are three.

It's also true that certain words sound funny; certain words don't. It's like that wonderful scene from Neil Simon's "Sunshine Boys" when Walter Matthau tells Richard Benjamin, "I know what's funny. Words with a 'k' in them are funny. 'L's are not funny—'M's are not funny."

On this subject of comedy. What's a "button"?

Marcia: It's the finale. The little piece of business that is not necessarily written into the script. As the talent reaches the end of the spot an ad lib might just happen. That's called the "button." Sometimes the button is written into the spot. Other times the writer hopes the talent will put a button on it. It's not always an ad lib.

You can't just go into the booth and wait for an inspiration. It's something you should think about while in the waiting room. Sometimes you're working with someone you know and funny things just happen. That's great. But for me, so much of comedy is planned out, crafted. If you're looking at a piece of copy you can't just go in and say, "Oh well, I think I'll do it three ways," and then hope you're going to think of the three ways while you're in the booth.

It's very frustrating when you come up with something funny at an audition. You do it and you don't get the job. Then you hear the spot on the air with someone else using your ad lib. There's no way around it. I think you have to give a little to get back a little. I'm always willing to go in and throw in my ending because maybe that's what's going to make them remember me just a little bit differently.

What is your attitude when you go out on an audition?

Marcia: It's not a negative to want a job. It's an imperative. But I don't walk into an audition and say, "I'm better than anyone else in this room." I don't feel that. I just feel I'm here and in a very positive attitude and I'm going to get this job. I don't want to sound arrogant, but you are dealing with a profession in which you must put yourself on the line daily for almost every job you do. So you have to go in there with a positive attitude and mind set.

It's not, "Oh my gosh, I need this job." Because then you say, "Oh damn, I didn't get this job." To me, it's like being an athlete. The athlete says, "Okay, there is no problem. I am confident. I am going to win this tennis match." It's that "personal best" feeling. You must really feel good about yourself when you go in for something. You must like yourself. You have to feel good even if you feel lousy. You must be that good actress and say to yourself, "All right, for ten minutes I'll feel good!" The most important thing is to enjoy and love what you are doing. And I do.

Don Peoples, Actor

Don Peoples was born about half way between World Wars I and II and grew up in New York. He was offered an announcing job at the Armed Forces Radio Network in Germany, but he was already writing for *Stars and Stripes*. For most of his adult life Don was a copywriter at three major ad agencies. In 1981 he crossed over and went on to become one of the leading and more versatile voice-over actors.

Don, do you think that your advertising background has helped you in this business?

Don: I wish advertising was a required course for anyone thinking about a career in commercial acting. Over the long haul it gives you an edge. Of course the hardest part of making the switch was unlearning directing skills. I mean, just take direction and perform. No second-guessing. It took me about three years.

Don, how easy are dialects?

Don: To be able to speak dialects you have to understand language. You have to know that certain sounds are endemic to certain people and places. The *n* in French is totally different than the *n* in German, which is totally different than the *n* in Russian. It doesn't mean that you have to speak any of these languages. But you sure as hell have to know how to get from the airport to the hotel and order a few meals.

The problem is that many people who write for dialects aren't expert in dialects. Add to that, the people for whom you audition who aren't knowledgeable about dialects. So, let's say you're called in to do French. You must be prepared to do the real French sound, the cartoon French sound, the educated French sound or a street sound. If it's CHerman, do zey vant zee storm trooper, vitch iss in zee opper nasal voice vit an ottitude. Or a hoz-frau, country-CHerman zimple zound?

For any dialect to work you must be lucky enough to be blessed with the "ear" and the ability to connect the ear to your vocal chords. It's organic. I don't think it can be learned.

What are some of your do's and don'ts?

Don: Learn to use your own voice first, before you do anything else. If you have one sound and you do one thing, do it the best way you can. If you have hundreds of sounds, remember they can't all be the best. Learn to recognize your strengths and weaknesses.

Learn your microphones. Talk to engineers about microphones. Your best friend in the voice-over business is not a) your mother, b) the casting director, c) your agent, or d) other actors. It is your engineer. Learn from him, work with him.

Listen to the radio. Listen to television. If you possibly can, when you make the rounds of agents, ask to listen to some of their client reel. Get to know what the competition sounds like.

Never bad-mouth another performer. It's a very small business.

A well-written commercial has a rhythm. It's musical. If it's not in the script, create and put it in your delivery.

Whether you're talking to another person in a dialogue spot

or talking directly to the audience, remember you are talking to one person. Approach that script as if only one person is your audience. Visualize that person. Know who he is and direct your copy to him.

Don't read your script aloud in audition waiting rooms.

Brad Abelle, Actor

Brad was born in St. Louis, Missouri, and was raised in Kansas City, Kansas. Currently based in Atlanta, Georgia, he is a staff announcer for Turner Network Television (TNT). His voice can be heard on TBS, CNN, Headline News, SportSouth, and numerous other television stations. In addition, Brad provides many of the NFL's and NBA's promotional announcements for TNT. He has done commercial voice-over work for *The New York Daily News*, Hardees, Macy's, Kroger, and Blue Cross-Blue Shield. His industrial narrations boast clients such as Coca-Cola and Southern Bell.

A veteran of the New Jersey Shakespeare Festival, Brad holds a bachelor of arts degree in theatre from Drew University. Not too long ago, Brad left a successful voice-over career in the New York market and moved to Atlanta.

Brad, why the move?

Brad: Well, I've spent about eight years in New York and was considered "successful." I mean, top agent and network accounts. But I really felt the pace was getting to me and my family. So, since I had been in Atlanta before and knew the market to a degree, I decided to test the waters. Coming back to Atlanta, even after I had worked in New York, there was no guarantee that people would instantly hire me for work.

In fact, a couple of people said to me, "Just because you worked in New York, that's fine. But let me hear your demo reel. Maybe we'll consider you."

What do you think was the toughest part of the transition?

Brad: The fact that Georgia is a Right-To-Work state.

What is a "Right-To-Work" state?

Brad: A Right-To-Work state means that producers don't have to give preference to professionals or preference for employment to union members. They can hire non-union announcers or actors just as readily as they might a union member, without any reprisals. There's a large non-union talent pool in Atlanta. So one of the traumas of adjusting to this market after working in New York was dealing with producers who say, "Well, I'll just get a non-union guy who'll do this for less money." That was hard to swallow after working on all those network accounts. So what I did was a selling job. "Well, here's why I'm better than non-union guys. Listen to my demo reel. Here are my credits. Here's my experience." And I just sold from that standpoint. Eventually, the career took off here, like it did in New York.

A lot of people say that if you can make it in New York, you can make it anywhere. I believe that if you can make it as a union person in a Right-To-Work state you can make it anywhere.

Did you find your New York connections helped you in Atlanta?

Brad: I don't think a lot of people were terribly impressed with that, and, in fact, some were a bit alienated by that down here. I remember a couple of audio engineers here at a studio said to me, "Well, I suppose you've come down here to show us how to do it." That's not my attitude. I focus on doing a good job wherever I am.

Is there a difference in the auditioning process?

Brad: There's relatively little auditioning here. It's direct bookings, based on demo reels or word of mouth. In New York, everything is an audition. Here, I'd say it's rare to have an audition for anything. The talent pool is much smaller, so it's less of a headache to choose. In New York, Chicago, and Los Angeles, you might have hundreds of guys who are good, dozens who are great. It makes it harder to choose.

Do you find there's a level of difference in creativity?

Brad: I think this town has some rising stars. But I would say that the majority of the nationally recognized work is still coming out of Los Angeles, New York, Chicago, Minneapolis, and San Francisco, for example.

How did you become a staff promo announcer for TNT?

Brad: When I learned that TNT was looking for a male promo announcer, I called the promos department and said, "Hi, my name is Brad Abelle, you don't know me, but I'd really like a shot at this thing." To make a long story short, I did get an audition. Two months later, I got a second audition, and then one month after that, I got the job. It's timing, persistence, determination, and networking. The talent had to be there, but I don't think that's what got me in the door. I think *chutzpah* is what got me through the door.

Are there differences between doing promo sessions and doing standard 30- or 60-second commercials?

Brad: At TNT, I record an hour a day. I can do up to 15 different pieces of copy in an hour for up to seven or eight producers. You have to be a quick study. Often, I have to read the copy cold and I have to do it right on the first, second or third take, give them what they want, be highly directable, and move on, otherwise the material won't get done. Whereas doing one 30-second commercial, a producer will often use the entire hour. So you have to be very quick. You do the voice track, and the producer runs with it to a post-production house, stays there all night putting voice to picture and then it's on the air, often the next day. Very quick turn-around time. I do six one-hour sessions a week, two on Wednesdays.

Do you work to picture?

Brad: No, and that's something that I wish we did. When I do promos, none of them are ever done to picture. You're flying blind. You really have to draw a picture in your mind, or, at least, ask the producer what's going on visually. In fact, I'll ask questions like, "What is the music track like? Describe it to me. What's the mood of the spot?" What they tell me helps me put the voicing together for the promo.

I think my New York experience definitely helped me here. Because I learned how to work fast. I learned how to take direction. I learned how to be versatile and imaginative mainly because of the auditioning experience in New York. So I've definitely taken all that great stuff I learned in New York and funneled it into my work with TNT.

What are the toughest sessions for you?

Brad: I would have to say the sports promos, which tend to have a hard-driving kind of read. The toughest is doing multiple takes for sports and then doing non-sports promos. I ask to do the sports reads last. That saves my voice.

I find it challenging doing so many pieces of copy in an hour. But even with time constraints, I've often stopped myself in the middle of a read and said, "Well, that really isn't right. Let's do another one." Or I'll say, "Well, I hope you're pleased with what we've done. But may I please try one more? I'd like to try something else." What I learned in New York was that producers really like an actor who doesn't come in and stand there like a robot, but really brings something to the session. I tell you, more often than not, the take that I ask to do extra my own way is often the buy. I don't think that means that I'm a better director, but it's just another perspective and they give me the freedom to do that.

What advice would you give someone who wants to make the same type of move you did?

Brad: I would say learn your market. You have to be humble, patient, and willing to start over in many ways. You have to start your sales efforts all over again. It's hard work, but it can pay off. Other advice? I guess it's the same all over. Market yourself, be persistent, follow up, be professional, be on time, be courteous, don't burn any bridges. Just do the best job you know how to do. Let the rejections roll off and move forward to the jobs you do get.

One aspect of settling in a market outside of New York, Chicago, and Los Angeles is that there are very few network spots produced. A lot of the work is local or regional. It's more of a volume business. The saving grace is that it doesn't cost nearly as much to live outside those major markets. Check out your new market thoroughly—agents, talent pool—talk with producers, look into housing costs, etc. My wife, my son and I are enjoying our life here.

Joyce Reehling, Actor

Joyce Reehling's career is not limited to voice-over and on-camera performing. She has been a guest star on many television shows like "The Days and Nights of Molly Dodd," "Kate and Allie," and "The Equalizer" as well as a featured role in "Another World." She just finished a run in the Broadway hit "Prelude To A Kiss." Joyce has been a member of the Circle Repertory since 1975.

When not performing in New York, she frequently returns to her alma mater, North Carolina School of the Arts, and teaches a commercial class to theatre students. She says it's her way of giving back some of what she has learned, and is still learning, about an industry in which she is a first-class contributor.

Since you do on-camera and voice-over, which do you prefer?

Joyce: If I could make a steady living in voice-over and radio, I'd never go back to on-camera. So far the industry is not clamoring for someone on-camera in my age bracket which is twenty-two to twenty-four. Okay, I lied. I'm plus or minus forty. And it's a very difficult age for a woman. It shouldn't be—it's wrong, it's stupid, it's all those things—but the business really starts separating you out at that point.

I started moving into voice about five years ago. I enjoy it. I like the people better. It's not 8 to 12 hours with a committee of 16 going, "Could she lift and push the thing a little closer, but stress the word 'cookie'—meanwhile, could you stir with your foot while you stand on your head . . . ?"

Not that long ago, I did an on-camera for a cream cheese. There were 50 things flying in the air. Toast popped out of the toaster and I had to catch it in mid air. So they said, "Oh, don't look at it. Don't look to catch it. We want everything flying through the kitchen and you should catch the stuff but don't look as if you're planning to catch it." It was a horrible day. I mean it was a horrible day.

I can walk into a studio for a radio spot or a voice-over and usually I'm out in an hour. You tend to be treated better. I like a modicum of respect. (Call me a fool.)

There are a handful of casting people and studio people who, when an actor walks in to do a job, are ready, willing, and able to just allow your creative juices to flow. Under those conditions, an actor can really do the work. So often the frustration of the business is that you walk in and they're not ready, they don't know what they want. And since they have no place to go with their particular feelings of inadequacy, or their not knowing what they want, they start ragging you. But if the atmosphere is right, an actor can get to exercise a lot of choices within a 30-minute period.

Okay, but haven't you gone in to do a voice-over or a radio spot and encountered the committee?

Joyce: Yes, but it's worse on-camera. Because what they're niggling about is the light hitting the clock in the back. I've done some film work. They don't spend that much time on whether this flower is being lit. Or, "Gee we go past that chair and there seems to be a nick on the back of it. Do you think they'll see it?" But you know what I mean? They niggle and piggle over things in a 30-second spot that nobody is ever going to see anyway. They have to justify why 35 people are sitting there going, "Uh-huh." You get it in voice-over, too. But, then again, half the time when I've worked voice, I can usually say to them, "Here's what I'd like to do. Can you let me do three takes, three in a row each, no comments?" And usually, they'll give it to me.

Is that at an audition or at a booking?

Joyce: At a booking. If the copy is short enough, I like to do three in a row, a few times, with decent feedback. A lot of times you get someone who doesn't know how to talk to an actor.

I went to an audition yesterday. It was funny copy, very well written. The writer and the casting person were in the room. It was a two-character piece. One person talking to the other, on the phone. It was a car rental situation. Now, my choice was to slow it down a bit. This was in order to lay out the sell points in the copy. Now basically, all the writer had to do was say to me, "That's the right approach. We need the pacing faster." Just tell me if I'm heading in the right direction. But instead, she began reading the copy the way she wanted it. She really wanted to read her own copy. Now the woman's reading was monotone and uninteresting. Finally, I said, "Excuse me. So what you're saying to me is you like the attitude but you need it faster?" She said, "Yes." And I said to myself, "We've just wasted two and a half minutes of her time and my time." She probably didn't know what to say. Or she's not cutting loose of the ego.

The nice thing about instant re-play on something you've done, is that if you can hear back something they like, then you can keep playing it back in your head until you give them what they want. And it will color itself differently through sheer repetition.

Something occurred to me while I was working on a piece of copy at a session. So often I hear people reading copy as though it's different from acting. I guess over the years of theatre work and high imagination work—you know, building an inner life, an off-stage life, a real existence for someone who has to come on and do maybe only two minutes on stage—what I find is that the best readings I do are those where I create that inner life. Somehow, when I'm reading copy I'm getting a picture or I'm putting myself in a place. It's second nature.

I guess if I was going to offer insight to someone, if they're coming from the theatre, it would be, don't be afraid to let that technique come through. Good acting is good acting. You learn to compress it, condense it. I think voice commercials are a skill more than an art form. It doesn't mean that it's not as good. Skill is skill. But if you can bring to it the texturing you do and the imagination, over a period of years it just kicks in. And what helps me get from take to take is that I stay true to the character.

Now, the problem is if someone is being really unclear with me in either an audition or a session, then I may have to take the bull by the horns and say, "All right, now let's talk about who this person is," without sounding like Uta Hagen on a bad day. I've got to get them to tell me about this character. What they say is, "Well, I want it faster—and it's got to be real funny." You can't act funny. You can't do funny. If copy isn't funny, you can't make it funny. What you can do is try to come from some character point of view. And if you're working with another actor, really work with the other actor. That rhythm between the two of you will sometimes create the illusion of humor where there is none.

Part of what you have to learn is not to overwork the copy in your head. Don't sit there trying to make all your decisions. I'd go through it. I'd mark it. I'd try to hear it in my head. But guess what. When you walk in there and you do your first reading they go, "No, it's really not what we had in mind, you'd better be able to adjust. Drop it and get on to another direction, which is what you should do in the theatre as well. But this is faster and it's for money. And they're interested in, "Can you deliver it in 60 seconds?" "When I say funny, can you get funny?" "If I say, 'Can you try that again, only this time with a sense of irony?' " You get all these mixed messages. They'll say things like, "I really want her to be forceful and just on the verge of anger but with a real softness and warmth and a sense of humor to her." Well, you can't do that. So you have to try to sift through the garbage and find out what this person is really saying. These people should all come with interpreters.

When you get into the booth with another actor, or even with the copy, let the moment carry you and feed you ideas. If you go in so frozen, cause you've memorized the piece of radio copy (which you don't have to do), you don't get that play between you and the microphone or you and the other actor. During performance, there is no safe way. You're going to have to take the risk of being wrong. And that's very scary. That's what rehearsal is for.

If I say one thing to people when I teach at North Carolina School of the Arts, it's this: I don't audition ever, any more. I stopped auditioning eight years ago. I rehearse in front of people. An audition implies judgment. Of course I'm at an audition. But for me in my head, if I can think of it as rehearsing, it gives me a lot more freedom. It also gives me the illusion that I actually have some control of the situation.

I don't hesitate to turn around and say, "All right, let's put one down." Because the minute you say, "What do you want me to do with it?" they'll say, "I don't know, what do you want to do with it?" So, if I put one down, they're either going to say, "That's great" or "Gee, we really weren't thinking along those lines." Then I can say, "Okay, along what lines were you thinking?" So now we have a dialogue from which to begin.

Not long ago, someone who is not in the business, asked me my definition of a good director. I said, "I can tell you what a bad director is. If you imagine you're on the limb of a tree. A bad director is huddled against the trunk of the tree, you're out on the limb and he's pushing you out saying, 'Could you just go to where it gets thin out there? Go to the twig. I think it's in that direction.' A good director is one who is walking with you, slightly behind you saying, 'Let's find it together.' And a great director gives you the illusion that he's already on the twig saying, 'Come over here. I think you're going to like it.' And for him, you run."

When I do my teaching, I invariably get students saying to me, "I don't need commercial work, I'm going to be doing theatre and I'll never need this." Or, "I'm going to work in the repertory companies. I'm not going to need to be in New York." I say, "Excuse me, where do you think they cast from? They cast from New York." Meantime, while he's in New York trying to book this repertory job at the age of twenty-two, how many roles are there? What about rent? Expenses? Extra money on which to get by? It doesn't fall from the skies. If it weren't for commercials, I would not have the theatre resume I have. I couldn't afford to stay in it. I thank God for commercials.

As a serious actress, do you feel demeaned by commercial work?

Joyce: I think if you're an actor and you only work the theatre, you're in a constant state of being demeaned by the fact that you can't make a living. And I don't want to live on $400 a week for the rest of my life. That means you can never go on vacation. You have to buy new shoes and clothes every other year. God forbid you get married and get pregnant. How do you raise a kid? Gosh, even baby Reeboks cost $30, $40 bucks!

It's funny. Poverty and struggle looked real amusing up until about the age of 30. And from 30 to 35 they lost their charm. And when you're careening into 40 you're saying, "I don't want any of that anymore. Where do I sign the part where it says I get money?" I've been able to do Broadway, Off-Broadway, and new plays sheerly by the fact that my rent was paid by commercials.

What would be some of your do's and don'ts of the voice-over industry?

Joyce: You have to work it like a business. It's not show-art. It's called show business. It's keeping a schedule, keeping yourself disciplined. It starts with the simple things. Keep a good date book. Return calls. Especially casting calls. Call either way. Yes, you'll make the audition. No, you can't make it, thank you. Never walk away from a call.

There are people in the cities where commercials are cast and produced, and you should ask working actors who they are, or read this book and find out where to go for coaching in this field. If you're a well-trained actor you'll probably be able to move into this pretty easily as far as technique and style. But don't go to somebody who doesn't do it. Not even the best theatre coaches, unless they're working this side of the business, can teach it.

Be on time. Unless you've been kept late at a previous call, always show up on time. No drugs. No alcohol. You don't sleep around with people in the business. Keep your nose clean and have a happy life. You don't get the work by doing favors. You earn what you get.

MICHAEL MISLOVE
(See page 119)

NELLIE BELLFLOWER
(See page 119)

MARCIA SAVELLA
(See page 125)

DON PEOPLES
(See page 131)

BRAD ABELLE
(See page 133)

JOYCE REEHLING
(See page 138)

JACKSON BECK

(See page 145)

RALPH BELL

(See page 152)

JOYCE GORDON

(See page 156)

JUNE FORAY
(See page 163)

MASON ADAMS

(See page 167)

15
Legends

It was both a privilege and a joy (I was giddy, even!) having the chance to talk with these particular five professionals, whose cumulative years in this business total over 230. The interviews with Jackson Beck, Ralph Bell, Joyce Gordon, June Foray, and Mason Adams are interviews filled with some insights, some bittersweet memories, some joys, and a couple of great laughs. For who they are and what they have contributed to the industry, I respect them. For allowing me to probe and poke into their yesterdays, todays and tomorrows, I will always be grateful. My advice to you, the reader: Savor each page—then reread, learn and apply!

They are the reason I named this chapter, *Legends*.

Jackson Beck

From the beginning of his radio career, Jackson Beck has had the distinction of working on the air for almost every small radio station in New York City, Brooklyn, the Bronx, and Queens. He did acting mostly, some announcing, producing, and directing. His first network job was "Death Valley Days," followed by "Myrt and Marge," on which he played the juvenile romantic lead.

It's safe to say that in the world of voice-overs, Jackson Beck, at some time, has done almost everything. Today you can hear him doing sports promos for NBC, as well as a myriad of commercials from Little Caesar's Pizza, Kellogg's Frosted Flakes, and Honey Graham Crackers to the voice of the engine in the AMOCO spots.

Jackson, how many years have you been at this?

Jackson: Sixty. I've been an actor for 60 years. I started in 1931 in radio. I know my business and I know my English. And I guess I have a certain latitude because of my position and my experience. People will listen to me. When I correct grammar, believe me, it will then make sense. I feel that I have a responsibility because people listen, especially kids. I do a lot of kids' stuff, and my audience is pretty young. If I make a mistake, those kids copy me and they make a mistake. And then it goes on from there.

You say kids are your audience. What particularly do you do that is directed at kids?

Jackson: Well, I've done a great number of children's shows and a great number of commercials directed at children. And they do pay attention.

This is embarrassing. Do you have a demo reel?

Jackson: Absolutely. A salesman carries samples. I'm proud of what I do. If there's something there that satisfies me I want it on a reel to show what I can do. I think every client has a right to understand what he's buying. And if he likes me, fine. And if he doesn't, tough.

But everyone knows you. You are the king!

Jackson: They only find out they know me after they hear the reel. Then they say, "I've been listening to you ever since I was a kid."

Do you carry this reel around? Gee, you must get a hernia.

Jackson: I don't carry the reel around. But I send it to whoever requests it. A producer will call me. I think he has a right to go to his client and say, "This is the voice I want." And so my reel has widely different treatments of different copy so that whatever happens to come close to what the client has in mind, he'll buy. He has every right to do that. I wouldn't go into an automobile showroom without trying four different models of a car.

How does it feel to be a real legend?

Jackson: That's other people's perception, not mine. I'm a working actor. And I treat it as a business. If somebody thinks I'm really marvelous, fantastic, or whatever the hell they happen to think, and some of them think I stink, that's all right with me. I don't mind it. But I don't pay any attention to it. Because that's somebody else's perception.

A lot of casting people are young and don't know how to direct talent. How do you deal with that when you come across it?

Jackson: When I'm in a casting office and being told the wrong thing, I won't do it. Here's a classic example: I was called in to read for a product. The word "environmental" came up. And I said it the way it's spelled. And the producer stopped me and said, "enviramental, pronounce it that way." I said,

"No I won't." I got my hat and coat and started to walk out. He realized he was incorrect. The session continued. By the way, this was not an audition. This was the booking.

Jackson, I know you are active in the unions. Could you enlighten the reader as to how they function?

Jackson: I've been a union man all my life. Not because I had to be, but because I wanted to be. It's a mark of professionalism. The union exists so that the people who work in any given industry or for any given business are not subject to exploitation by an employer or by management.

An employer will naturally try to get people to work for him or her at the lowest possible price that they will accept. Sometimes this is so low that the person can't make a living, can't live, can't have any extra cash around to spend. The function of a union is to get a wage scale up to an acceptable figure affordable by management and supportive of the worker.

This has two effects: 1) If every employer in a given industry is unionized, then the basis of competition which is at the base of business, the best product for the lowest possible price, obtains. That means that you can't undersell the other guy by cutting the worker's wage. It stabilizes an industry; 2) It gives a working person enough of an income to live decently.

If you're starting out in this industry, remember it's not an art. It's not a science. It's an industry. And its business is to sell products. That's my function. I don't always think of myself as an actor, but rather as a salesman. And my job is to move carloads of products and clean the supermarket shelves or whatever. That's my function. And without me and people like me, business goes to hell in a bucket. If we're not out there to sell that product competitively and get a decent share of market, we're all failures. So I'm a salesman primarily. That I happen to sell a character or a voice and, incidentally, a product, is really beside the point. The point is to sell. That's what this country is founded on. That's what it will always be founded on. That's the name of the game.

As far as actors joining unions, I believe in it. It's the mark of professionalism to carry the union card. Yes, unions do have faults. We are trying our best to correct them.

For those of you who do not know how this industry works, let me explain. You do a job. That is not the end of it. It's the use of that job that you get paid for, where you really make your money.

If you don't work every day, but a commercial you did weeks ago is still running, you are still selling the client's product. He has to pay you. But if you have no way of checking, you're never going to get paid for it. The union helps keep the cheap-jacks out of business.

In my day, we started in small radio stations and we learned our trade, our craft. That opportunity is not readily available these days.

"It's a bird—it's a plane—it's SUPERMAN!" Eight of the most famous words ever spoken. And you, Jackson Beck, are the man who said them!

Jackson: I still speak them. Everybody wants to hear me do it when I go into a studio. Little did I know when I got on that show that it would be a career. Others had done it before me. But I guess, fortunately, I got tagged with the identity.

For how many years were you the radio announcer for "Superman"?

Jackson: Let's see. I started in about '42 or '43 and I went on with it until it finally ended sometime in the '50s. Then we went on to do a cartoon series of "Superman," also "Superboy." I guess I got about 15 very productive years.

Has the commercial auditioning and booking process changed a lot over the years?

Jackson: No. Well, I have to interpret that two ways: The general process of auditioning and getting the job has not changed. My personal experience has changed because now people call me directly sometimes. They write things that call for my particular treatment of copy. I don't treat all copy the same way. I'm loud, I'm hard, I'm also soft, and I'm also one-on-one.

Of course, there are very many aspects of this process of interpretation. Some people wouldn't hire me for a hard-sell job on a bet because they like the soft stuff I do. And the reverse is true. Some would never consider me for a cosmetic sound because they think of me only as the voice of time. And don't forget, I played one of the most romantic parts that was ever on radio. I did "The Cisco Kid." I was Cisco—with all that soft, romantic, Mexican accent. And on "Superman," I played Beenie, the office boy, and every heavy that came along as well as every dialect that you could think of. I did Bluto on "Popeye." And on Saturday morning cartoons, I'm King Leonardo. (I don't get up that early on the weekends to watch it.)

I found out something. Characters come and go, but the announcer is there every day. Announcing is only another phase of acting anyway. You're either an actor or you're not. You are born one. The only way to learn is by doing. So do as much as you can, wherever you can.

I have to give you a couple of words of warning. If you're going to get into this business, remember something. This is really not to deter you, because if you've got a dream and you've got the talent and you've got some experience, go after it. But you are facing 60,000 experienced people. That's your competition. You'd better be damned sure that you know what you're doing. You have to have knowledge, experience, sensitivity, some talent, and you have to be able to interpret the English language. You have to understand what the writer is trying to say. And if he can't say it, you take that piece of cotton and make it into silk. But there are 60,000 people out there already who can·do it. And you're up against a tough road.

This is not just reading off paper, *believe* me. You should be able to interpret at sight, do cold readings and make them sensible, and you must have a sense of timing. If you are in there with a piece of copy and you have 28 and four-tenths seconds in which to do it, you damned well better know how to do it. Because if you run 28 five, you've got to do it again. If the copy runs short, you have to stretch. And then you have to stretch without sounding like it. So you change your style, you change your delivery. You're not born with that.

Also, if it's too long, you've got to know how to shave off two-tenths of a second and not sound like you're rushing. You only get that through experience. I don't know where you're going to get it. But you'd better find out. This is not an easy business. It's true that I can walk in (and so can 5,000 of my compatriots) and knock off 10 spots within an hour. And I have seen some other people take 10 hours to do one spot.

I've been in this business all my life. I'm not just an announcer, I'm a marketer. I am an advertising man. I know this business inside and out. You've got to know the other side of this business. You must know the market you're trying to reach because it affects your delivery. You are picking out a segment of the demographic whole. You have to appeal to the segment to which the commercial is directed. Over the years, I've picked up all these things. You're going to have to know all this going in, because you're up against me.

Ralph Bell

Ralph Bell was born in New York, grew up in New Jersey, and attended the University of Michigan in Ann Arbor. From college he came to New York and was there about three months looking for work as an actor. During those years, the Antoinette Perry auditions were held to discover new performers. Actors had the opportunity to perform part of a one-act play at a Broadway theatre, to which agents and producers were invited. During one of these searches, Ralph was given the chance to direct a one-act play. As a result, he was offered jobs as a director, and to this day, he still loves directing. In the recent past he has directed about a dozen plays, some new, in regional theatres.

His first acting performance was as a walk-on in a George Abbott production. Eventually he worked up to being an understudy and then into real parts. It was at this time that Ralph also got into radio by doing dramas like "Gang Busters," and "FBI in Peace and War," as well as a formidable list of soap operas. He calls those times the halcyon days. As he so aptly put it, "It was a way of life, the passing of which I mourn."

Then came live television. Ralph performed as well as wrote for television. Because of his extensive radio experience, he moved into voice-overs as a natural progression.

Clearly, Ralph Bell has one of the most identifiable sounds in voice-overs. You've heard him on Andersen Windows, Carefree Gum, Western Union, Milk Bone Dog Biscuits, Shadybrook Farms, Shreaded Wheat, and I'm running out of breath.

You have what is classically known as a quirky or unusual sound. How has this contributed to, or taken away from, your success?

Ralph: All I can comment about that is when people mention this, with an overuse of modesty I say it took me 40 years to ruin my voice so that it became commercially viable and the quirkiness is because of erosion.

Maybe part of why I have survived is because, allegedly, I am an actor. I've done 13 Broadway plays, a few Off-Broadway plays, and, in the heyday of radio drama, I was fairly active. I don't put any emphasis on voice at all, although I do have a way of extolling a product but with a certain gentle skepticism.

It's the copy. It is what is inventive about what is written down, the concept. It's my job to interpret it. If I have any pride at all, it would be in my ability as a technician, an interpreter. I think I am a pretty good actor and I am able to reflect what is in the copywriter's head when he puts it down on the page. I get meaning very often, where there is no overt meaning.

How do you feel about the young crop of casting people at agencies?

Ralph: I don't really know how they get their jobs. To me it seems like the traditional start would be in the mail room and go from there. So these young people are assigned to be buffers. To be a buffer, you have to kind of elevate your position. So there's an air of superiority. After all, they are in the arena of employing people, screening them. And so the attitude can often be, if they have a chip on their shoulder, rather unpleasant at times.

It amuses me when I encounter it. It can bother and hurt a lot of people emotionally, particularly if they're just starting out in the business. You're selling yourself. That's the toughest part of all.

Because your voice marries to copy, do you and your agent discuss what you should be submitted for—with what you want to be identified?

Ralph: The agent really knows what I have a flair for. I have a way of sounding amusing. If the copy has a comic element to it, usually they will submit me for it.

Ralph, some advice—some dos and don'ts.

Ralph: You must realize in the beginning that what you're entering is the arena of rejection. Now the idea is to really adjust to that. You're not going to win every audition. You're going to be very, very lucky if you win one, or a call back on one. The experience can be very bruising if you let it really affect you. Nobody likes to be rejected. But you've chosen this particular hot kitchen that you've entered. And if you are really going to pursue this thing, the best way you can protect yourself is to shrug it off. You'll win one if you've got any talent at all and then that will generate others. But don't take it as a personal affront. That's my main attitude.

Here's something—let's say you've won the audition and now you are at the session. If there are more than six people on the committee listening to you, it may be tough. Because six people have six different opinions—some of them quite valid—some of them just trying to contribute to save their jobs. But a committee of over six could result in a rough session. Sometimes it doesn't happen. It's a matter of keeping your cool when you're doing it. You're going to be assailed with all kinds of suggestions. Most of them will make sense, particularly if the writer is there. He has a concept and you were chosen to reflect that concept. And there are times when you're not really fulfilling the idea—or the sound—he had in mind. So, you'll be directed. And sometimes that can be very, very confusing.

Just remember, you were hired because what you were doing in the audition fit the concept. So you're ahead of the game really. The annoyance or what may get to you is, "Do it again, do it again, do it again." This is particularly true if you're working to picture. That can be very tricky.

Can you explain what makes recording to picture tricky?

Ralph: Certain words or portions of the copy must often sync, or fit, with key moments of the visual. Unless you have a facile memory, reading from a script and looking up at the television monitor in order to fit the words to the picture can make for a tight navel. Often there may be too many words in the copy. The technique is to make it all fit without it seeming to sound rushed. Sometimes it is impossible. If the director or writer is experienced, he can cut or substitute a word or phrase to achieve the desired effect of getting the information across without losing the impact. The whole process can sometimes have an element of tension, particularly since all this must happen within the usual hour of studio time.

But you learn by doing. Again, always remember that if you don't do it within the time allotted, there is an engineer there. If these people at the session are experienced, they know very well that one take can be adjusted to another take. The engineer can help you. Don't feel diminished if you don't do it all in one take. Rely on the fact that there are professionals involved in this process. The main thing is keep a sense of humor about it.

You are active in SAG. What is your title?

Ralph: I'm a member of the board now. I have served previously as a vice president of the New York branch, also as president of the New York branch. When you serve on any of these boards, there is always an element of politics. There are politics also in arriving at decisions. I'm not particularly interested in that.

Basically I am a very firm and devout union man as far as Screen Actors Guild is concerned, because without SAG or a union it would be chaos. Everybody would be hurt. The element of professionalism would be diminished, and also there is a regulation that does occur by the presence of a union. Everybody gets a fairly fair shake. Not only the advertising agencies but the performers as well.

In total, how many years have you been in this business?

Ralph: Well, figure it out—since 1938.

Joyce Gordon

Joyce Gordon was born in Des Moine, Iowa, and raised in Chicago. Her acting career began at age 12 on Chicago Board of Education radio dramas. She continued appearing on radio and on stage at The University of Illinois. She came to New York, transferred to Eastern University, and landed her first professional job on radio's "Counterspy." She has appeared on several thousand radio and television shows, including "Robert Montgomery Presents," "Studio One," "Edge of Night," and "Search for Tomorrow."

Joyce started doing commercials in the '50s on live television. She was the on-camera spokeswoman for Standard

Brands. Then she became the spokeswoman for Crisco and Duncan Hines, remaining so for over 10 years. Joyce established a unique identity by wearing her glasses on television. She was the first woman to do so, and they became her trademark.

Today, Joyce does only voice-over commercials. Besides commercials for AT&T, Prell, Jello, Minute Rice, etc., her voice is heard on countless promos for NBC programming, Home Box Office and Lifetime Cable Television.

She has dubbed countless foreign films into English under the direction of Sergio Leone, Jean Renoir, Rene Clement, and Henri Verneuil, and has become the voice of international stars Claudia Cardinale, Jeanne Moreau, and Annie Girardot. Her husband is actor Bernard Grant, and they have two grown children.

Do you think of yourself as an actress or someone who does voice-overs?

Joyce: I think it's important to establish one important aspect of my work and me. I'm an actress. People say—because everyone's so hip about the business now—"Oh, you're a voice-over," and I say, "No, I'm an actress who does voice-overs." And that's an important distinction.

Why do you say that?

Joyce: First of all, I believe that if you really look around, you'll find that the most successful people in the voice-over area are, indeed, trained actors, doing acting now, or having done it on television, radio, stage, or movies. Although some of us are good at announcing, we are basically actors. Being an actor gives you added insight into what you're doing as well as the versatility that helps keep you alive.

If you're going to be successful in any business, and, in

particular, our business, you have to have a combination of talent, intelligence, and discipline. Now talent is something you have. However, it can't just be left alone to blossom. You still have to study, learn, and develop it. Intelligence is something, hopefully, you were born with and you continue to use, and discipline is essential. By that I mean professionalism in your work habits.

What's a big "don't"?

Joyce: Don't get a big head. Don't think that if you're the hot person in commercials today, or in any medium, that's gonna last forever. Because everyone has hills and valleys. Vogues come and go, and you've got to develop many strings to your bow. I'll take my talent in any direction I can apply it.

During the early years, you made your own choices. You didn't need a commercial agent. It was a much smaller industry dominated by a few ad agencies. You could make rounds yourself. As the industry grew, an agent became indispensable. And I have always been exclusive with an agent. That was my choice. I've been at this since I was 18. Forty years, my dear.

People listen to you, in some way, every day and don't know it. What is the most famous pre-recorded line you utter?

Joyce: "I'm sorry, that is not a valid number." I'm under contract to Dun and Bradstreet. I'm Dun's voice—the voice of all their systems. The point is, you take your talent everywhere. We once bumped into an actor in Hollywood, who said to my husband, "Are you doing a lot in New York?" And I'll never forget his answer. He said, "We're doing a lot of a lot." And that's what you do in New York. A lot of a lot. A New York actor does some theater, some narration, some radio spots, some television commercials, an occasional series, gets a part in an occasional movie—a lot of a lot.

You have an incredible reputation in this business. How do you keep it together when you walk into a place where a casting person is less than knowledgeable?

Joyce: Oh, that happens often. And frankly, lately more of what happens is that they've never heard of me because they're young, and I understand it. I don't do a thing. I behave as I would under any circumstance. I don't say, "You mean you didn't know me?" or "I've done this or that." I'm there and I do the best I can, and I'm as nice as I can be, and do the best audition I can do. I have a theory about auditions. It's very important to give yourself every break in an audition. In other words, a lot of voice-over auditions are conducted without any storyboard, without any knowledge of what's on camera. I see people waiting to audition in the waiting room, and reading the copy and listening to themselves and practicing. If I get a script with no pictures that's clearly TV, the first thing I'll ask the casting director is, "What are the pictures?" And after they tell me, I'll ask, "Is there music with this?" And if so, "Do you know what kind of music it is?" In other words, give yourself every piece of information you can get in order to have a better understanding of what the commercial should sound like and what it is trying to say.

Also, at an audition or a session, if you feel it didn't go well, say so. "Please, I'm not happy with that. May I do that once more?" It's the only chance you're going to get. If you're given a script that has the video on one side and the audio on the other, read the video first. I always do that. It helps me better understand what's going to be on camera. That's going to tell me more than just reading the copy. It's conceivable that the copy could fit all kinds of pictures. I'll give you an example. I was at an agency. They'd had auditions going for three days, men and women. It was for an air conditioner. I walked in and the copy had no pictures and was totally technical. "This machine gives you this much BTUs," etc. Everybody was practicing and rehearsing. When I went in, I said, "What are the pictures?" Do you know what the picture was? The sexiest girl you've ever seen, caressing and sidling around an air conditioner. Now all the people outside who had been madly rehearsing had locked concepts in their heads and didn't know what the picture was. I got the job, by the way.

When I first started to do commercials, I was an actress only. I had never done them before. I was blessed to work with a guy who was marvelous, and he said to me, "What you must do immediately when you read a commercial is say, 'What are they trying to say? What are we selling?'" This may sound over-simplistic, but that is the key to it. Commercials aren't that complex. You must understand what you're trying to sell. Once you understand, you can do it in different ways to different pictures. But if you fail to understand that, you will never convey it properly. And the funny thing is that an actor works that way with a scene in a play, but many fail to work that way with a commercial. If any actor picks up a scene, he'll be taught to say, "What is my intention here? What is my objective? What is my relationship to this character?" They don't ask themselves the same questions when approaching a commercial.

I'm trying to say that if you do not know what you're talking about, you cannot do it as well. I once worked with a top guy and it wasn't going well. I had two lines; he had the whole thing. We had gone over it about 18 times, and the producer was worried that perhaps the copy wasn't clear. And he suddenly said to the actor, "Tell me what you just said." Now this guy had to read it 18 times. And he said, "Why, I just said . . . I-I-I." He stammered and stuttered. He finally had to look at the script to tell the producer what he'd been saying. Now that's my problem with people who sit in waiting rooms rehearsing how they're going to sound and how they're going to read something. The way I work is, I read something two times, three times tops, to get what it's all about. And then I put it aside. I don't want to over-rehearse it before I know what they have in mind. I don't want to form set ideas on how to read each thing. And most of all, I don't want to be listening to how I sound when I do it. Don't listen to how you sound! Think about what you're saying. Because if you're thinking about what you're saying, you're going to sound right.

It is my view that if you understand the copy—and it all begins with copy—then you should be able to give a reading of that copy, without direction, that is perfectly fine, effective, and clear. But you must also have the ability to complete a 180-degree turn and do it another way. I've seen actors nod to a director, "Yeah, yeah, yeah," and then read it again exactly the same way. So you need both. You need the ability and the intelligence to bring to the copy what it requires if there's no one to direct you, and the ability to respond to direction. And never lose sight that you are working for someone. If they ask you to do it again and again and again, don't get itchy and testy. Do it. That's your job. They're paying you to do that.

What are some of your other dos and don'ts?

Joyce: Well, the first "do" is to protect your voice. Although I have smoked during periods of my life, I will never smoke again, because I felt my voice thickening. And also, it had an enormous effect on my breathing. When you're doing voice-overs you have to speak a lot of copy in a very compressed period of time, effortlessly. That is hard to do it you cannot control your breathing well. When I stopped smoking, the engineers noticed it immediately, and so did I. My breath and voice control were far better. I also have a special secret. I chew gum all the time. Gum keeps you moist; lozenges don't. Gum helps you produce saliva and prevents dry throat.

The second 'do' is listen to what's on the air. Stay aware of what's going on and what's selling. The third is listen to yourself all the time and learn. In a session, one play back is worth a thousand words. So after a few takes, ask for a play back to hear what you are doing.

Some big "dos." Be on time, be cooperative, take direction, and be kind to your fellow performers. And don't forget your engineer. He is your best friend. Your engineer handles your voice on mike, helps move the sessions, and, in my case, often gets me more jobs than my agent. That's the truth. So remember them, know them, and thank them. My last "do" is a matter of choice. I wear "cans" or headsets when I work. It gives me a better handle on what I'm doing. It's a personal preference.

The "don'ts"? Don't think you're the hottest thing that ever hit the town. Don't make phone calls, over-socialize, or tell too many jokes in a session. It's a business and someone's paying for studio time. Observe the rules of the industry, i.e., don't take product conflicts when you shouldn't and don't violate any union rules. Finally, don't get glued to the page when you're working to picture. It is extremely important, in my view, to be able to get off the page and look at the picture. I have seen many people who are very good who never get off the page. They're the ones who go 32 takes. You must develop that technique of looking up and down so that you are seeing the picture as you are reading.

How would someone practice on her own if she's never done it before?

Joyce: Well, I would think that what you do is imagine a screen or someone in front of you, pick something that you want to read, even if it's a magazine article, and start reading it and looking up as much as you can, so that you learn how to read in phrases. It's what news people do all the time on television, when they're not using a Teleprompter. But you must develop that. In my opinion, you will never do superlative voice-over work if you're not capable of that. If you're not looking at the picture and listening to the track while you're reading, I submit that you're going to miss things that are going to kick off little nuances in your reading. It's the difference between okay and really good.

Don't try to manufacture a sound. I would say try to develop and stay within your own sound and your own talent. Don't imitate, don't be phony. In the long run it won't work for you. And the name of the game is the "long run." Hitting is one thing—lasting is quite another. That's the true test, isn't it?

June Foray

She has been called the "first lady" of off-camera voice actors. June is as legendary as the animation producers with whom she has worked.

Theatrically trained, June Foray did not plan to specialize in voices. She was working in Hollywood on stage, television, and film when Capitol Records put her under contract to do children's albums and comedy records with Stan Freberg. These led her to doing voices on Capitol soundtrack albums of Hollywood cartoons that were heard by The Walt Disney

Studios, which soon signed her to provide voices for characters in their films, including "Cinderella" and "Peter Pan." Warner Brothers also discovered her talents, and soon she was working in dozens of Warner Brothers shorts, most notably as Tweety Pie's Granny and as Witch Hazel.

When animation became a hit on TV, so did June Foray. She is currently Jokey Smurf in Hanna-Barbera's long-running hit series, "The Smurfs," Grammi Gummi in Disney's "Gummi Bears," Magica de Spell and Ma Beagle in Disney's "Ducktales," and Granny in Warner-Spielberg's "Tiny Toons." Although she has done hundreds of voices, most people identify her with the voice of Rocky, the Flying Squirrel. In fact, her collaboration with Jay Ward on the "Rocky and Bullwinkle Show" continues to bring her recognition: In 1986, she was honored in New York's Museum of Broadcasting's tribute to Ward's shows.

Because of her fame as a voice actress and her long-standing love for the art form, June Foray has been invited to speak on the art of animation all over the world—from Russia (where she is well known for being the voice of spy character Natasha) to France, Yugoslavia, Japan, England, Australia, and New Zealand, and, of course, across the North American map.

June currently is serving her fifth term on the Board of Governors of the Academy of Motion Picture Arts and Sciences and is also chair of the Academy's Short Films branch and co-chair of its student film awards committee.

In October 1990, June received the Pegboard International Award for her contribution to animation. It was presented by Association International Du Film D'Animation in Genk, Belgium.

How do you come up with a voice?

June: The artist draws what is called a "model sheet." You examine the type of character it is, and the director will explain, "Well, this is the attitude: young/old, contentious, ingenuous." You really have to think off the top of your head, "Well, how do you think this will work?" Then you try a voice. Sometimes it works and sometimes it doesn't.

How did you wind up doing cartoon voices?

June: I was in radio in the '50s while under contract to Capitol Records, along with Stan Freberg, Daws Butler, Mel Blanc, recording children's records. At that time, neither Warner's nor Disney had their record companies. As a result, we recorded all their animated shorts and features. As a matter of fact, I was playing the wicked queens, Alice, and all of the Disney characters. Disney listened to all this and said, "Why is this girl just doing records? She should be over here working." So the first thing I ever recorded was Lucifer the Cat in "Cinderella," two of the mermaids, and the Indian squaw in "Peter Pan," going on to do several shorts, including "Trick Or Treat," playing Witch Hazel. Chuck Jones over at Warner loved the Witch Hazel character. So he brought me to Warners to play Witch Hazel in "Broomstick Bunny" in 1954. Fortunately for me, they realized my versatility, and Friz Freleng hired me as Granny for "Tweety and Sylvester." I went on to perform in about 70 Warner Brothers cartoons.

Hanna and Barbera were still at MGM. So off I went and did a witch for them as well. Tex Avery, also at MGM, had heard about me. And so I was thrilled to record a couple of films for him.

Of all the characters you do, who is your favorite?

June: I guess it has to be Rocky and Natasha, because the dialogue was so brilliantly written. The satire was superb. It was mordantly witty. We offended everyone, but in a kind and gentle way. Because of the attraction it has for kids as well as adults who understand the jokes and all the outrageous puns, I guess I can't help but feel that way.

What advice would you give someone trying to break into the business?

June: Be absolutely certain that you have talent. Now, I know everybody thinks they have talent. But, I always say take your best friend to bed with you, and your best friend is your tape recorder. Talk into it, read copy, and let it stay two days. Then listen to it. If you have any intelligence at all, you will say, "That was pretty miserable" or "I have talent." Go to play readings, take classes with a competent teacher. But be careful. There are many people teaching who have no right to do so. Look for someone who has distinguished himself or herself in the industry. I taught at USC [University of Southern California] for seven years, but students who took my classes knew my professional background.

What are the big no-nos as far as you're concerned?

June: Being unprepared to read copy cold at auditions, or being inarticulate in communicating with directors. There is something for which actors entering the business must be prepared. Rejection. It's denigrating to be informed that your performance was not professional enough. Therefore, you must be absolutely certain that you have thick enough skin. When you're young and are sent out on auditions, you're full of high hope. You know you did one hell of a good job. But then you're rejected. You lie awake at night thinking, "What happened? What did I do? What didn't I do?" It's heart-rending and worrisome. Thick skins, as well as perseverance, are imperative.

Who are some of the "greats" you most remember?

June: Working with Mel Blanc at Warners was most rewarding, as well as recording comedy albums with Stan Freberg. It was exhilarating working with famous people like Chuck Jones and Friz Freleng, Tex Avery, Joe Barbera, and Bill Hanna. And then of course, associating with Jay Ward and Bill Scott on the "Rocky and Bullwinkle Show." It's a part of my life that I will never forget and for which I am extremely grateful.

Mason Adams

Mason: I knew I wanted to be an actor when I was five years old and was playing Humpty-Dumpty in a camp play. As I fell off the wall, I knew, by gosh, this is what I want to do. Anyway, I think most of us who are performers have been so since childhood. I learned the art of improvisation in elementary school, during a performance playing William Tell. I pulled the bow to shoot the arrow off my son's head, the bow broke, and there I was with all these parents looking at me. Panic! What the hell was I going to do?

What did you do?

Mason: A simple improvisation. I picked up the arrow and threw it.

When did you seriously pursue acting?

Mason: In high school. I was an avid fan of radio drama and I started writing radio plays in the style of then-current shows

like "The Witch's Tale" and "The Silver Flute." I began performing these at school assemblies, playing all the roles, and
in the process, I acquired primitive performance skills which
I kept on sharpening and developing.

Two and one-half years into college, I decided I wanted
professional training. I won a scholarship to the Neighborhood Playhouse. I studied there for a year. Then, at my parents' urgent request that I arm myself to earn a living in some
way, should acting fail, I went back to college. I got a master's
from the University of Wisconsin, prepared myself to teach,
and did teach. I taught at the Neighborhood Playhouse, the
Dramatic Workshop, and various other places.

When did your career begin?

Mason: I started working in the theatre in New York in the
mid-'40s, and at the same time began to move into radio. Initially, I was contemptuous of radio acting. I viewed it as a
minor skill compared to theatre. But it turned out to be in-
finitely more. I was able to combine working in theatre and
radio. And radio became a major part of my life. Early on I
won the role of Pepper Young on "Pepper Young's Family"
and stayed with that into early 1960, when it went off the air.
All through that period I did a number of Broadway plays
and hundreds of radio shows.

Some years ago, I was asked to speak at a Radio Advertising
Bureau Convention on my work as a radio actor. I said, "In
the words of that famous Dutch philosopher Xaviera Holland-
er, 'It wasn't work, it was a pleasure.' " And so it was. Radio
was that much fun. You ran around from show to show doing
all kinds of parts. Those were great days.

Along about 1960, dramatic radio began to disappear. A lot
of actors went out to California, hoping to do film work. I
elected to remain in New York, and knowing that theatre

wouldn't support me, and realizing that I had to find something beyond radio that would provide a regular living, I started auditioning for and doing radio and television commercials. That's how I became a commercial spokesman.

Initially, I kind of looked down on the whole business of doing commercials, just as I had originally looked down on radio. But you change your views, and now I not only don't look down on them, I really enjoy doing them. But it's a different medium. It's a different technique and it takes different skills. And it's equally demanding.

As a commercial spokesman, my specialty has always been voice-overs. I've never done on-camera dramatized commercials.

Explain the difference between a dramatized on-camera spot and an on-camera spokesman?

Mason: In a dramatized on-camera spot, you play a character. As an on-camera spokesman, you are simply yourself, promoting a product or service. That is something I'm always happy to do, providing I approve of what's being sold. Of course, voice-over work, because of its anonymity, is the preferred work in the television and radio commercial field—the one most people go after.

This is true. But you, Mason Adams, are not anonymous.

Mason: My voice is unquestionably recognizable. I don't know whether that's good or bad. And I won't deny that I do enjoy being recognized, both vocally and physically. But it does have its drawbacks. If I act like a horse's ass in public, as I sometimes have been known to do, I feel more than normal guilt afterwards.

You did a soap opera. What motivated you to do it?

Mason: The producer, at the time I did it, had a passion for using first-rate Broadway actors. I was flattered to have been asked. And for the brief period during which I did it—I went from it into "Lou Grant"—I worked with a whole bunch of fine actors and directors.

In which of the media do you prefer working?

Mason: It's kind of like the lyric from "Finnian's Rainbow": ". . . when I'm not near the girl I love, I love the girl I'm near." Whatever I'm doing, I enjoy it while I'm doing it. Each discipline has its own pleasures and requires its own set of skills.

Mason, some advice to people starting out in the commercial business?

Mason: There are several things that I would recommend. The first is, if you have the money, check out the people who hold classes. At the very least, you will have an exposure to the material, exposure to your peers, you may be able to create a reel for yourself, and it gives you an introduction to the field. I would also recommend constant reading aloud. Whatever the material is—a daily newspaper, editorials—simply pick it up and read it out loud. The practice is invaluable.

Contrary to what people might think, you don't need an agent to work in New York City. In California, you do need one. In New York, get lists of the various casting people and send out your demo reel. Most of them will listen to it. Casting people are always looking for a new sound. If you can get just one audition, you're really moving up. The whole business of auditions is, to me, the name of the game. Because every time you audition, somebody new hears you. Somebody may just zero in and say, "That's the quality I'm looking for." The likelihood of it happening, of course, is remote—one in a hundred. But it's a one-in-a-hundred business. But that's the way to build a career in this business. If a copywriter happens to listen to an audition session, and even though you may not have been picked for that job, the next time something comes up, he could say, "Hey, what about that person from the last audition?" That's the way the business works.

What advice would you offer an actor going to an audition?

Mason: Get hold of the copy and go to the bathroom. Work on it alone. Don't sit with your fellow actors and shoot the breeze. Go work on the copy. Become familiar with it. You can't do that in the presence of others. I think socializing at one of those large auditions can be poison. Because by the time you get inside, you've forgotten the material and your concentration isn't on it. Zero in on what you are going to do. Have a plan and a program. Do it out loud. Reading the material to yourself doesn't give you the chance to hear what you're doing. That's another reason why finding a private place to read is the only way. You can't read aloud in the waiting room. Another thing: Underplay the material—less is more. Make it conversational. Take those words and make them sound as if you own them. That's not easy to do. And never, ever, feel superior to what you're doing. It'll show and you're history.

I have to mention Smucker's. I must. Your voice and that product are a perfect marriage. How do you feel about being so identified with a product?

Mason: I can't help but enjoy it. It's been so many years and I'm so fond of everybody involved—Lois Wyse and the people who work with her, the Smucker family. They are a wonderful group.

There is a great story about Smucker's. When I was first

on the account, the commercials were quite straightforward. The agency had been trying to convince the Smucker family that it would be good advertising to poke fun at their name. In some parts of the country, their name was an ethnic joke. The idea was met with resistance until finally, at a directors meeting, a 90-year-old aunt in the family asked: "Will it increase the dividend?" The answer was, "Yes." She said, "Do it." And that's how, "With a name like Smucker's, it has to be good" emerged. The success has been phenomenal. Of course, their products are wonderful. But so is their advertising. So we've been together all these years, and it's been a very happy association.

How many years has it been, Mason?

Mason: Close to 30 years.

Do you still have a demo reel?

Mason: Sure. And a demo reel can be very important. For example, from time to time I have been offered accounts simply on the basis of that reel. So yes, demo reels can be extremely important.

Memo

TO: You, the reader
FROM: Me, the writer

Throughout the book, I have suggested that you send your demo reel to agents, casting people, agency people, and production houses. But where can you reach them? I've researched and come up with some sources you may want to look into:

Ross Reports Television
4029 27th Street
Long Island City, NY 11101
(718) 937-3990

Among its many publications is a monthly edition of *Ross Reports* in which are published lists of New York City talent agents franchised by the three performing unions, SAG, AFTRA, and EQUITY; New York City independent casting directors; New York ad agencies that have in-house casting; New York producers of television commercials, New York and Los Angeles dramatic serials, formerly known as soap operas (including casting and production staff); and New York and Los Angeles network prime-time programs (including casting and production). I was told that the list for Los Angeles casting for primetime programs is strictly informational. They work with agent submissions only.

Twice a year, Ross Reports Television publishes *Ross Reports, USA.* This is a guide to talent agents and personal managers nationwide. (It lists both National Conference of Personal Managers and Conference of Personal Managers.) They inform me that this publication is not a duplication of "Ross

Reports Television." The franchised agents in this guide are listed geographically. New York is excluded.

I found them to be very friendly and helpful on the phone. They are knowledgeable and willing to share their information.

Peter Glenn Publications, Ltd.
17 East 48th Street
New York, NY 10017
(212) 688-7940 or Toll Free 800-223-1254 or Fax (212) 752-5972
Of their various publications, I chose *Madison Avenue Handbook*. Published once a year, this spiral-bound indexed directory is geared toward the advertising and communications industries. Included are names, addresses, and phone numbers of ad and public relations agencies, marketing, production and post-production companies, and talent agencies throughout the United States, and lots more.

This handbook might be overkill for someone just starting out, in which case you might want to get Peter Glenn's *NYC Casting & Survival Guide,* available with or without the date-book. This book is for the performing artist and contains information on schools and teachers, pictures and resumes, casting in New York and Los Angeles, and talent reps.

My conversation with Peter Glenn Publications employees was pleasant and informative. They were eager to help. You might want to call or write to them and find out what else they offer.

Motion Picture Enterprises Publications, Inc.
Tarrytown, N.Y. 10591
(212) 245-0969 or FAX: (212) 245-0974
Of MPEP'guides, the *Audio Visual Source Directory* gives you a

direct hit on audio visual houses throughout the country, broken out geographically, and good sources for audio tape duplication. It also covers much of what you don't need, but the cost of the book is low. It's worth it for the A/V list alone.

These people were also kind and helpful.

Henderson Enterprises
360 East 65th Street, 15E
New York, NY 10021
(212) 472-2292
Thanks to Gina Makowski at William Morris for this one. Henderson Enterprises sells mailing labels, supposedly up-dated and checked monthly, of all casting directors and agents, both theatrical and commercial, broken down by in-dividual market. You can buy them by the specific market or in any combination.

The company also sells lists of children's agents, modeling agencies, photographers, soaps, etc. The prices are pretty rea-sonable and vary depending on the number of labels in the particular category.

Breakdown Services, Ltd.
1120 S. Robertson, 3rd Floor
Los Angeles, CA 90035
(213) 276-9166
Basically, this is a Los Angeles-based service that provides lists of all studios and independent production companies with casting breakdowns of the various productions being filmed throughout the country. It also offers various direc-tories and mailing labels. Pertinent to your needs would be casting directors on Rolodex-cards, available for New York or Los Angeles, cross-indexed by individual and company name.

You can get mailing lists of Los Angeles or New York casting directors, both geared toward theatre, television and feature films; Los Angeles commercial casting directors, either independent or associated with a production company or advertising agency; Los Angeles SAG franchised agents, and New York agents.

The people at Breakdown Services were not as easy to speak with as those at the other companies. But, who knows, maybe they were having a bad day.

Back Stage
330 West 42nd Street, 16th floor
New York, NY 10036
(212) 947-0020 or FAX: (212) 967-6786
Most of you should be familiar with *Back Stage*, a weekly trade publication based in New York and distributed to major markets, including Los Angeles, Chicago, and Washington, D.C. *Back Stage* also includes regional columns targeted to Florida, Chicago, Los Angeles, the Northwest, Texas, and Boston.

In addition to its weekly trade paper, in 1989 they introduced *Back Stage Handbook For Performing Artists*. Published every two years, it's a compilation of articles that appeared in *Back Stage* that were of interest to the performer, e.g., where to get pictures and resumes, how to select the right photographer for your head shots, or where to find agents, casting directors, as well as work opportunities for actors, singers, and dancers in theme parks, cruise lines, summer stock, cabaret, and stand-up comedy.

Write or give them a call. I have had only good experiences with everyone with whom I've been in contact over at *Back Stage*.

Shakespeare Mailing Service
311 West 43rd Street
New York, NY 10036
(212) 956-MAIL (212) 586-1267 fax

I found a real 'find.' (Did that make any sense?) They specialize in the preparation and mailing of any and all promotional material for actors. They keep computerized up-to-date lists (up-to-date is the operative phrase) of NYC agents and casting directors. The lists clearly identify who handles the various areas of business—theatre, film, television, commercials, voice-overs, print and industrials. They will work with you 'one-on-one,' helping you determine how you can best use the promotional materials you already have or whether you might need different materials to achieve your objectives. Shakespeare prepares resumes and also handles postcard and headshot reproduction.

For corporate clients, such as casting directors and producers, Shakespeare helps keep them in touch with the media and industry contacts that contribute to their success.

I would have to say that the secret to Shakespeare's success is its president, Hal Hochhauser. He is dedicated, caring and available. Even if you're not sure what you might need, give Hal a call. He's a wonderful person with whom to 'troubleshoot.'

It doesn't hurt to remind you to keep up with your local trade papers. You will always find bits and pieces of information and advertising directed to all areas of the performing arts.

16 Don't Give Up Your Day Job..........

Wouldn't it be ideal if every actor wore a big sandwich sign with **"Fragile, Handle With Care,"** printed in boldface type, as a constant reminder of the oh-so-fragile ego? I guess casting people could wear that same sign. While we're at it, what about writers? Producers? My gosh, what about an entire world where everyone's primo concern was . . . everyone else? Okay, so it ain't going to happen. So let's look at how we, in this ego business, can survive. Heck, never mind survive. Let's flourish!

It's essential that you think of yourself as a business. Yes, you heard me. That is exactly what you are: a small, service business with something to sell, your talent. So, have a quick board of directors meeting with yourself and vote to get your ass in gear.

1. Separate yourself from your service. It's the hardest thing to do, but you must do it. Step out of your fragile ego and accept that if you don't get the booking for a voice-over job,

it is you, the voice, that didn't get the booking, not you, the person.

2. Target your selling efforts. For example, in sending out your demo reel, instead of covering every single casting director listed, do a little research. As I'm sure you are aware, there are those who cast for soaps, film, and television. Find out who casts for radio and television voice-overs. For starters, send your tape to just that group. Congrats, you've just saved your company time and money.

3. Keep good records. I don't mean just financial records but good follow-up records. Any time you do a mailing, keep a checklist as to whom you sent what and when. If and when you get any response, record it in your checklist. Any input you get should be noted. Keep an appointment book. If you get an audition, write down the name of the person who sent you in, the person you saw at the audition, the name of the place at which you auditioned, the product, and, if possible, the agency.

4. Do something to advance your career every day. Any small company must do self-promotion. Besides mailings to casting directors who do radio and television voice-overs, there are small production companies that do non-broadcast narrations. Local cable companies do promos or, as they are sometimes called, *next-ons*, for upcoming programs, e.g., " 'Gone With The Wind,' next on Cablevision." "Stay tuned for more antics from those frolicking, funny folks from 'Night Court'—next on Cinecable."

5. Don't give up your day job. I mean that. This is one business that affords you the latitude of getting a foothold before you let go of your security blanket, your day job. You get the best of both worlds—a steady paycheck while you're learning a new profession.

6. Never act needy or desperate. Don't place too much importance on any one audition or any one job. It's hell on your head and no good for your soul.

7. Without question and at all costs, maintain your sense of humor. This should be a fun business. I mean look what you get to do. As a grownup, you sometimes get to make silly sounds with your voice. You can create characters, give life to inanimate objects. Make people laugh. Make people cry. It takes about an hour. And you get paid well for it! It's not so bad. It's also not the answer to world hunger or a cure for cancer. So, keep things in perspective.

8. Never bad-mouth a casting person or an agency producer. It's a small business. Rumors, good and bad, travel quickly. It's oh-so-easy to be labeled a troublemaker.

9. Be gracious and generous with your fellow performers. Certain people are all too eager to see you fail. (One less voice-over in the competitive ring, right?) Don't give anyone any reason to dislike you.

10. Don't be afraid to make mistakes. Make them all. You're allowed. Make them big. Don't be tentative. Make your mistake as if you know what you're doing because who knows, maybe you've guessed right! And make them once. Making the same mistake more than a few times shows you haven't learned from them.

A good number of years ago, my friend, Henry Hoffman, introduced me to a book that has become my personal reference book. My employees have read it, and I speak its praises at all my lectures. Besides the book you now hold in your hands, what could be so wonderful? *How To Win Friends & Influence People* by Dale Carnegie. Our industry is a people industry. In addition to having talent, timing, and luck, you must understand people: from the people for whom you audition to those you ultimately reach with your voice. I urge you to pick up a copy of the book. Read it and apply some of the techniques. They work, I swear it. (My favorite story is about the fisherman and the strawberries and cream.) Although this book is just about finished, my help for you isn't. If any of my explanations were unclear, or if you have a question that I didn't address, write to me. I will answer, I promise. In addition, if you want me to listen to and evaluate your demo reel, send it to me. Wait two to three weeks before you call me. And be prepared, because I will tell you what I think. Send everything to:

Alice Whitfield, President
Real-To-Reel Recording, Inc.
303 Fifth Avenue, Suite 409
New York, NY 10016
Tel: (212) 889-1557

If you would like me to respond to your letters, please make sure you print your name, address, apt. number, city, state and zip — so I can read them.

Okay. It's time. Enough reading. Carry *Take It From The Top!* with you. It will fit right next to your appointment book. You just have to get out there and give it a shot. Ask a lot of questions. That's how you'll learn. My Dad used to say: "Alice, if you throw enough things up to flypaper, something's gotta stick!" Get out there and start throwing. It works. My Daddy said so. And . . . break a leg!

17
A Big Head Start

Most of you know about *Backstage*, *Variety*, and the *Ross Reports*. Among other things, they provide you with the names of agents, independent casting companies, production companies, and open calls.

The following is a selected list of advertising agencies that do a lot of voice-overs, both television and radio. I've divided them into regions. Since staff turnover changes hourly, address your material (tape and cover letter) to one of the following: Head of Broadcast Production or Creative Director or Casting Director. Go get 'em!

AGENCIES IN THE EAST

AC&R Advertising, 16 East 32nd Street, New York, NY 10016
Al Paul Lefton, 71 Vanderbilt Avenue, New York, NY 10169
Ally Gargano, 805 Third Avenue, New York, NY 10022

Altschiller Reitzfeld Davis/Tracy-Locke, 1740 Broadway, New York, NY 10019

Ammirati & Puris, 100 Fifth Avenue, New York, NY 10011

Avrett, Free & Ginsberg, 800 Third Avenue, New York, NY 10022

Backer Spielvogel Bates, 405 Lexington Avenue, New York, NY 10174

Baldi, Bloom & Whelan, 41 Madison Avenue, New York, NY 10010

Bennet Book Advertising, 60 East 42nd Street, New York, NY 10165

Berenter Greenhouse & Webster, 233 Park Avenue South, New York, NY 10003

Bergelt/Litchfield Raboy Tsao, 345 Hudson Street, New York, NY 10014

Berton Miller Associates, 135 Fifth Avenue, 3rd Fl., New York, NY 10010

Biederman Kelly & Shaffer, 100 Fifth Avenue, New York, NY 10011

LKW/Eric Mower & Associates, 96 College Avenue, Rochester, NY 14607

Bozell, 40 West 23rd Street, New York, NY 10010

Brouillard Communications, 420 Lexington Avenue, New York, NY 10017

Burson-Marsteller, 230 Park Avenue South, New York, NY 10003

Cajun Films, Inc., 36 East 20th Street, New York, NY 10003

Calet Hirsch & Spector, 250 Park Avenue South, New York, NY 10003

Campbell Mithun Esty, 405 Lexington Avenue, New York, NY 10174

Carafiello Diehl, 90 N. Broadway, Irvington, NY 10533

Carelli, Glynn & Ward, 1250 Route 23, Butler, NJ 07405

Chalek & Chalek, 380 Lexington Avenue, New York, NY 10017

CHC Advertising, 1480 Route 9N., Woodbridge, NJ 07095

Chiat Day Inc., 79 Fifth Avenue, New York, NY 10003

Communications Diversified, 440 Park Avenue South, New York, NY 10016

Cooper-Cameron Inc., 1283 Broad Street, Bloomfield, NJ 07003

Crowley, Webb & Associates, 37 Franklin Street, Ste. 200, Buffalo, NY 14202

D'Arcy Manius Benton & Bowles, 1675 Broadway, New York, NY 10019

David Deutsch Associates, 655 Third Avenue, New York, NY 10017

DCA Advertising, Inc., 1114 Sixth Avenue, 32nd Fl., New York, NY 10009

DDB Needham, 437 Madison Avenue, New York, NY 10022

DDF&M Inc., 200 First Avenue, Pittsburgh, PA 15222

DellaFemina McNamee, 350 Hudson Street, New York, NY 10014

Della Femina, McNamee, 600 Grant Street, Pittsburgh, PA 15219

Dick Jackson Inc., 160 East 56th Street, New York, NY 10022

Direct Response Broadcasting Network, 1101 Market Street, Ste. 1300, Philadelphia, PA 19107

DMB&B, Inc., 909 Third Avenue, New York, NY 10022

Doremus, 1633 Broadway, New York, NY 10019

Dresner Sykes Jordan & Townsend, 168 Fifth Avenue, New York, NY 10010

Drossman, Lehman, Marino, Revely, 80 Fifth Avenue, 6th Fl., New York, NY 10011

Earle Bower Associates, 1220 Broadway, New York, NY 10001

Earle Palmer Brown, 257 Park Avenue South, New York, NY 10017

Earle Palmer Brown, & Spiro, 1 Liberty Place, Philadelphia, PA 19103

Elkman Advertising, 150 Monument Road, Bala-Cynwyd, PA 19004

FCB/Leber Katz, 767 Fifth Avenue, New York, NY 10019

Foltz/Wesinger, Inc., P.O. Box 1297, Lancaster, PA 17603

Geer DuBois, 114 Fifth Avenue, New York, NY 10011

Gene K. Kolber Advertising, 500 N. Easton Road, Willow Grove, PA 19090

Gianettino & Meredith, 788 Morris Turnpike, Short Hills, NJ 07078

Gilbert, Whitney & Johns, 110 S. Jefferson Road, Whippany NJ 07981

The Gillespie Organization, Inc., International Corporate Center, P.O. Box 3333, Princeton, NJ 08543

Godfrey Advertising, 2890 Hempland Road, Lancaster, PA 17602

Gray Baumgarten Layport, Inc., 2275 Swallow Hill Road, Pittsburgh, PA 15220

Grey Advertising, 777 Third Avenue, New York, NY 10017

Griffen Bacal, 130 Fifth Avenue, New York, NY 10011

Group Two Advertising, Inc., 2002 Ludlow Street, Philadelphia, PA 19103

Hal Riney, Inc., 100 East 42nd Street, New York, NY 10017

Hallmark Advertising, Inc., 2 Chatham Center, Pittsburgh, PA 15219

Hank Forssberg, Inc., Two University Plaza, Ste. 208, Hackensack NJ 07601

Hart/Conway Inc., Eastman Place, Rochester, NY 14604

HBO, 120 East 23rd Street, New York, NY 10010, Attn: On Air Production

Hicks & Greist, 220 East 42nd Street, New York, NY 10017

Hill Holliday, 885 Third Avenue, New York, NY 10022

Holland & Calloway, 767 Third Avenue, New York, NY 10017

Hood, Light And Geise, Inc., 509 N. 2nd Street, Harrisburg, PA 17101

Hutchins/Young & Rubicam, 400 Midtown Tower, Rochester, NY 14604

ICE Communications, Inc., 2290 East Avenue, Rochester, NY 14610

Horowitz Marshall, 141 Fifth Avenue, New York, NY 10010

J. Walter Thompson, 466 Lexington Avenue, 2nd Fl., New York, NY 10017

Jay Incorporated, 912 Sibley Tower Building, Rochester, NY 14604

Johnson Films, 140 East 39th Street, New York, NY 10016

Jordan McGrath Case & Taylor, 445 Park Avenue, New York, NY 10022

Kelly Michener, PO Box 959, Lancaster, PA 17603

Ketchum Advertising, Inc., 220 East 42nd Street, New York, NY 10017

Ketchum Advertising, Inc., One Independence Mall, Philadelphia, PA 19106

Ketchum Advertising, Inc., Six PPG Place, Pittsburgh, PA 15222

Keyes Martin, 841 Mountain Avenue, Springfield, NJ 07081

Koehler Iversen Inc., 71 West 23rd Street, #1505, New York NY 10010

Kolker Talley Herman, 171 Madison Avenue, New York, NY 10016

Korey Kay & Partners, 130 Fifth Avenue, New York, NY 10011

Laurence Charles Free Lawson, 260 Madison Avenue, New York, NY 10016

Lawrence Butner Advertising, 228 East 45th Street, New York NY 10017

Leo Burnett Company, 950 Third Avenue, New York, NY 10022

Lev Lane Advertising, 1 Belmont Avenue, Bala-Cynwyd, PA 19004

FCB/Lewis Gilman & Kynett, 200 S. Broad Street, Philadelphia, PA 19102

Lieberman-Appalucci, 4635 Crackersport Road, Allentown, PA 18104

Lintas New York, 1 Dag Hammarskjold Plaza, New York, NY 10017

Lois/GGK, 650 Fifth Avenue, New York, NY 10019

Lord Densu, 810 Seventh Avenue, New York, NY 10019

Lowe & Partners, 1345 Sixth Avenue, New York, NY 10019

Margeotes Fertita & Weiss, 411 Lafayette Street, New York, NY 10003

Martin Marshall Jacomma & Mitchell, 41 Madison Avenue, New York, NY 10010

McCaffrey And McCall, 575 Lexington Avenue, New York, NY 10022

McCann Erickson, 750 Third Avenue, New York, NY 10017

Miller Advertising, 71 Fifth Avenue, New York, NY 10003

NW Ayer, Worldwide Plaza, 825 Eighth Avenue, New York, NY 10019

Ogilvy & Mather, 309 West 49th Street, New York, NY 10019

Partners & Shevak, 1350 Sixth Avenue, New York, NY 10019

Pedone & Partners, 909 Third Avenue, New York, NY 10022

Rapp Collins Marcoa, 475 Park Avenue South, New York, NY 10016

Rosenfeld, Sirowitz, Humphrey & Strauss, 111 Fifth Avenue, New York, NY 10003

RRN & E, 100 6th Avenue, New York, NY 10014

Rumrill-Hoyt, Inc, 60 Corp Woods, Rochester, NY 14623

Saatchi & Saatchi Advertising, 375 Hudson Street, New York, NY 10014-3620

Saxton Communications Group, Ltd., 124 East 40th Street, #1101, New York, NY 10016

Scali McCabe Sloves, 800 Third Avenue, New York, NY 10017

Serino, Coyne & Nappi, 1515 Broadway, New York, NY 10036

Seth Berkowitz Productions, 14 East 38th Street, New York, NY 10016

Severin & Aviles, 328 East 61st Street, New York, NY 10021

Sheldon Fredericks, 71 Vanderbilt Avenue, New York, NY 10169

Slater Hanft & Martin, 111 Fifth Avenue, New York, NY 10003

Smith Greenland, Inc., 555 West 57th Street, New York, NY 10019

Solin Associates, 25 West 39th Street, New York, NY 10018

Sudler & Hennesey Consumer Group, 1180 Sixth Avenue, New York, NY 10036

TBWA, 292 Madison Avenue, New York, NY 10017

Ted Barkus Company, Inc., 1512 Spruce Street, Philadelphia, PA 19102

The Eagle Ad Agency Inc., 371 North Avenue, New Rochelle, NY 10801

The Bloom Agency, 304 East 45th Street, New York, NY 10017

The Stogel Companies, 19 West 44th Street, New York, NY 10036

The Weightman Group, 1818 Market Street, Philadelphia, PA 19103

TSR, 411 Lafayette Street, New York, NY 10003

Van Brunt & Company, 300 East 42nd Street, New York, NY 10017

Venet Advertising, 245 Fifth Avenue, New York, NY 10016

Waring & LaRosa, 909 Third Avenue, New York, NY 10022

Warwick Advertising, 875 Third Avenue, New York, NY 10022

Wells, Rich, Green, 9 West 57th Street, 16th Fl., New York, NY 10019

Winner Communications, 37 Union Square West, New York, NY 10003

Wunderman Worldwide, 575 Madison Avenue, New York, NY 10022

Y & R Advertising, 285 Madison Avenue, New York, NY 10017

AGENCIES IN NEW ENGLAND

Altman & Manly, 1361 Elm Street, Ste. 408, Manchester, NH 03101

Arnold Fortuna Lane, 420 Boylston, Boston, MA 02116

Cabot Communications, One Constitution Plaza, Boston, MA 02129

Charnas, Inc., 76 Eastern Boulevard, Gastonbury, CT 06033

Clarkegowardfittsmatteson Inc., 535 Boylston Street, Boston, MA 02116

Cosmopulos, Crowlley & Daly, 250 Boylston Street, Boston, MA 02116

Cronin & Company, Inc., 655 Winding Brook Drive, Glastonbury, CT 06033

Decker Rickard, 99 Citizens Drive, Glastonbury, CT 06033

Devine & Pearson, Inc., Crown Colony Office Park, 300 Congress Street, Quincey, MA 02169

Donahue, Inc., 227 Lawrence Street, Hartford, CT 06106

Doremus/Boston, 855 Boylston Street, Boston, MA 02116

Duffy & Shanley, The Penthouse, Providence, RI 02903

Fitzgerald & Company, Inc., 1 Worthington Road, Cranston, RI 02920

HBM Creamer, Inc., One Beacon Street, Boston, MA 02108

HBM/Creamer, Inc., 800 Turkshead Building, Providence, RI 02903

Higgins, Inc., 338 Newbury Street, Boston, MA 02110

Hill Holliday Connors Cosmopolus, 200 Clarendon Street, Boston, MA 02116

Houston Effler & Partners, 360 Newbury, Boston, MA 02115

Ingalls Quinn & Johnson, 855 Boylston Street, Boston, MA 02116

Keiler Advertising, 304 Main Street, Farmington, CT 06032

Leonard Monahan Lubars & Kelly , 127 Dorrance Street, Providence, RI 02903

MacDonald Boyd White, 286 Congress Street, Boston, MA 02210

Mariani Hurley Chandler, 42 Weybosset Street, Providence, RI 02903

Mason & Madison, 23 Amity Road, New Haven, CT 06525

Mintz & Hoke, 40 Tower Lane, Avon, CT 06001

North Castle & Partners, 300 First Stamford Place, Stamford, CT 06902

Pagano Schenk & Kay, 1 Old Stone Square, Providence, RI 02903

Rossin Greenberg Seronic & Hill, 181 Newbury Street, Boston, MA 02116

AGENCIES IN THE SOUTHEAST

Abramson Associates, Inc., 1275 K Street, NW, Washington, DC 20005

Advisors, 8200 W. Sunrise Boulevard, Ste. D-2, Ft. Lauderdale, FL 33322

Anson-Stoner Inc., 111 East Fairbanks Avenue, Winter Park, FL 32789

Halperin & Co., 3333 Peachtree Road, South Tower, Ste. 230, Atlanta, GA 30326

Austin Kelley Advertising, The Palisades, 5901 Peachtree Road, Dunwoody Road NE, Atlanta, GA 30328

Awareness Internat'l Advertising, 1628 E. Atlantic Boulevard, Pompano Beach, FL 33060

Babbit & Reiman Advertising, 3060 Peachtree Road, Atlanta, GA 30305

Barker Campbell Farley, 240 Business Park Drive, Virginia Beach, VA 23462

BBD&O, 3414 Peachtree Road NE, Atlanta, GA 30326

BD&A, 4600 Dundas Drive, Greensboro, NC 27407

Beber Silverstein & Partners, 3361 SW Third Avenue, Miami, FL 33145

Bouvier Kelly Inc., Seven Oak Branch, Greensboro, NC 27407

Brumfield-Gallagher, Inc., 3401 West End Avenue, Nashville, TN 37203

Buntin Advertising, Inc., 1001 Hawkins Street, Nashville, TN 37203

Burrell Advertising, 100 Colony Square Building, Atlanta, GA 30361

Carden & Cherry Advertising, 1220 McGavock Street, Nashville, TN 37203

Cochran & Sandford, Inc., 1400 Clark Tower, 5100 Poplar Avenue, Memphis, TN 38137

Cole Henderson Drake, 400 Colony Square, Ste. 500, Atlanta, GA 30361

Davis & Phillips, Inc., 121 College Place, Norfolk, VA 23510

DDB Needham, 8300 Greensboro Drive, Ste. 1200, McLean, VA 22102

Earle Palmer Brown, 1 East Cary Street, Norfolk, VA 23219

Ehrlich-Manes & Associates, 4901 Fairmont Avenue, Washington, DC 20814

Eisener & Associates, 12 West Madison, Baltimore, MD 21201

Eric Ericson Advertising, Inc., 1130 Eighth Avenue South, Nashville, TN 37203

Fahlgren Martin, 1 Paces West, Ste. 1800, Atlanta, GA 30339

Finnegan & Agee, 100 West Franklin, Richmond, VA 23220

Fitzgerald & Co., 11 Piedmont Center, Ste. 910, Atlanta, GA 30305

Fouts & Son Advertising/Promotion, Inc., 2405 Westwood Avenue, Richmond, VA 23230

Fry/Hammond/Barr Inc., 600 E. Washington, Orlando, FL 32801

Garber, Goodman Advertising, Inc., 4500 Biscayne Boulevard, Miami, FL 33137

Gold Coast Advertising, 3625 NW 82nd Avenue, Ste. 404, Miami, FL 33166

Good Advertising, Inc., 5050 Poplar Avenue, Memphis, TN 38157

Group 3hree Advertising Co., 3200 NE 14th Street Causeway, Pompano Beach, FL 33062

GS&B, 4104 Aurora Street, Coral Gables, FL 33146

Harris Drury & Cohen, 6360 N.W. 5th Way, Ste. 300, Ft. Lauderdale, FL 33309

Hawley Martin Partners, Inc., 1703 Parham Road, Richmond, VA 23229

Henderson Advertising, 60 Pelham Pointe, Greenville, SC 29615

Henry J. Kaufman & Assoc., 2233 Wisconsin Avenue, NW, Washington, DC 20007

Howard, Merrell & Partners, 8521 Six Forks Road, Raleigh, NC 27615

Hume Sindelar & Associates, Advertising/Marketing, Inc., 2500 SW Third Avenue, Miami, FL 33129

Husk Jennings Overman, 50 North Laura Street, Ste. 2600, Jacksonville, FL 32202

Jan Gardner & Associates, Inc., 3340 Poplar Avenue, Memphis, TN 38111

J. Walter Thompson, 950 East Paces Ferry Road, Atlanta, GA 30326

Kennedy Center Advertising, The JFK Center, Washington, DC 20566

Kerns & Associates, 1137 Edgewater Drive, Orlando, FL 32804

Ketchum/Atlanta, 2 Midtown Plaza, Atlanta, GA 30309

KSK Communications Ltd., 1577 Spring Hill Road, Ste. 600, Tysons Corner, VA 22182

Lewis Advertising, Inc., 1050 Country Club Drive, Rocky Mount, NC 27804

Loeffler Ketchum Mountjoy, 7401 Carmel Executive Park Drive, Charlotte, NC 28226

Leon Shaffer Golnick Advertising, Inc., 2817 E. Oakland Park Boulevard, Ft. Lauderdale, FL 33306

Leslie Advertising, P.O. Box 6168, Greenville, SC 29606

Lois/GGK, Merchandise Mart, Chicago, IL 60654

Long Haymes & Carr, 140 Charlois Boulevard, Winston-Salem, NC 27103

McKinney Silver & Rocket, 333 Fayetteville Street, Raleigh, NC 27601

McCann Erickson, 615 Peachtree Road NE, Atlanta, GA 30365

Michael Parver Assoc., 1819 Peachtree Road, NW, Ste. 333, Atlanta, GA 30309

M. Finkel & Associates, Inc., 1104 Crescent Avenue NE, Atlanta, GA 30309

Ogilvy & Mather, 1360 Peachtree Road NE, Atlanta, GA 30309

Price McNabb, 4600 Marriott Drive, Ste. 510, Raleigh, NC 27612

Richardson Meyers Donofrio, 120 West Fayette Street, Baltimore, MD 21201

R.J. Gibson, Inc., 11760 US Highway 1, Ste. 204, North Palm Beach, FL 33408

Spectrum Communications, 15 South Main Street, Ste. 700, Greenville, SC 29601

The Ad Team of Florida, Inc., 15251 NE 18th Avenue, North Miami Beach, FL 33162

The Blum Group, Inc., 17 Warren Road, Ste. 22-A, Baltimore, MD 21208

The Bomstein Agency, 2201 Wisconsin Avenue, NW, Washington, DC 20007

The Earle Palmer Brown Co./Atlanta, 100 Colony Square, Atlanta, GA 30361

The Martin Agency, 500 N. Allen Avenue, Richmond, VA 23220

Tracy Locke Atlanta, 4 Concourse Parkway, Ste. 225, Atlanta, GA 30328

Trahan, Burden & Charles, Inc., 10 W. Eager St., Baltimore ,MD 21201

Trone Advertising, P.O. Box 35565, Greensboro, NC 27425

Tucker Wayne/Luckie, 1100 Peachtree Road NE, Ste. 1800, Atlanta, GA 30009

Umphenour Martin Lonsdorf, 1315 Peachtree Road NE, Atlanta, GA 30309

Vansant Dugdale Advertising, The World Trade Centre, Baltimore, MD 21202

Van Winkle & Associates, Inc., 1819 Peachtree Road NW, Ste. 315, Atlanta, GA 30309

W.B. Doner, 2305 North Charles Street, Baltimore, MD 21218

Weitzman Livingston, 4709 Montgomery Land, Bethesda, MD 20814

West Pausback & Vaughn, 321 East Chapel Hill Street, Durham, NC 27701

William Cook Advertising, 225 Water Street, Ste. 1600, Jacksonville, FL 32202

AGENCIES IN THE MIDWEST

Bailey, Klepinger, Medrich & Muhlberg, Inc., 130 S. First Street, Ann Arbor, MI 48104

Bayer Bess Banderwarker, 225 N. Michigan Avenue, Ste. 1900, Chicago, IL 60601

BBD&O, 410 N. Michigan Avenue, Chicago, IL 60611

BBD&O/Detroit, 26261 Evergreen Road, Southfield, MI 48076

Bender Browning Dolby & Sanderson Advertising, 444 N. Michigan Avenue, Ste. 1400, Chicago, IL 60611

Bentley Barnes & Lynn, 420 N. Wabash, Chicago, IL 60611

Bernstein Rein, 4600 Madison, Kansas City, MO 64112

Bozell, 30600 Telegraph Road, Birmingham, MI 48010

Bozell, Butler Square, Minneapolis, MN 55403

Bozell, 625 N. Michigan Avenue, Chicago, IL 60611

Brainstorm Communications, 228 S. Wabash Avenue, Chicago, IL 60604

Brogan & Partners, 3000 Town Center, Ste. 475, Southfield, MI 48075

Burrell Advertising Inc., 20 N. Michigan Avenue, Chicago, IL 60602

Campbell-Mithun Esty, American Center Building, Ste. 1000, 27777 Franklin, Southfield, MI 48034

Campbell-Mithun Esty, 737 N. Michigan Avenue, Chicago, IL 60611

Campbell-Mithun Esty, 222 S. Ninth Street, Minneapolis, MN 55402

Carmichael Lynch, Inc., 800 Hennepin Avenue, Minneapolis, MN 55401

Case/Foley Sackett Inc., 708 N. First Street, Ste. 110, Minneapolis, MN 55401

Clarity Coverdale Rueff Advertising, 415 First Avenue North, Minneapolis, MN 55401

Clayton-Davis & Associates, Inc., 8229 Maryland, St. Louis, MO 63105

CMF&Z, 4211 Signal Ridge Road N.E., Cedar Rapids, IA 52406

Colle & McVoy, Inc., 7900 International Dr., Minneapolis, MN 55425

Cramer-Krasselt, Co., 733 N. Van Buren, Milwaukee, WI 53202

Cramer-Krasselt, Co., 225 N. Michigan Avenue, Chicago, IL 60601

D'Arcy Masius/B&B Inc., 1725 N. Woodward Avenue, Bloomfield Hills, MI 48303

Johns & Engel Inc., 343 W. Erie Street, Ste. 520, Chicago, IL 60610

DDB Needham, 303 East Wacker Drive, Chicago, IL 60601

Della Femina, McNamee, Inc., 500 N. Michigan Avenue, Chicago, IL 60611

Delleeuw Ferguson Bashaw Advertising, 210 South Woodward Avenue, Ste. 200, Birmingham, MI 48009

Dimensional Marketing, Inc., 211 E. Ontario Street, Chicago, IL 60611

DMB&B, Inc., 1725 N. Woodward Avenue, P.O. Box 811, Bloomfield Hills, MI 48303

DMB&B, Inc., 200 East Randolph Drive, Chicago, IL 60601

DMB&B, Inc., Gateway Tower, One Memorial Drive, St. Louis, MO 63102

Donald L. Arends, Inc., 1000 Jorie Boulevard, Oak Brook, IL 60521

Edward G. Dorn & Associates, Inc., 1801 "H" Hicks Road, Rolling Meadows, IL 60008

E. H. Brown Advertising, 20 N. Wacker Drive, Chicago, IL 60606

EJL Advertising/Chicago, Equitable Building, 401 N. Michigan Avenue, Chicago, IL 60611

Fallon McElligott, 701 Fourth Avenue South, Minneapolis, MN 55415

FCB/Chicago Inc., 101 East Erie Street, Chicago, IL 60611

Frank J. Corbett, Inc., 211 E. Chicago Avenue, Chicago, IL 60611

Garrison, Jasper, Rose & Company, Inc., 8440 Woodfield Crossing Boulevard, Ste. 280, Indianapolis, IN 46240

Goldfarb, Hoff & Company, 26250 Northwestern Highway, Southfield, MI 48075

Grant/Jacoby, Inc., 737 N. Michigan Avenue, Chicago, IL 60611

Griswold Inc., Landmark Office Towers, 101 Prospect Avenue, Cleveland, OH 44115

Harris West Advertising, 701 Fourth Avenue South, Ste. 1330, Minneapolis, MN 55415

Hesselbart & Mitten, 350 Springside Drive, Fairlawn, OH 44333

Hughes Advertising Inc., 130 S. Bemiston, St. Louis, MO 63105

J. Walter Thompson, 900 N. Michigan Avenue, Chicago, IL 60611

J. Walter Thompson, 600 Renaissance Center, Detroit, MI 48243

Jack Levy & Associates, Inc., 225 N. Michigan Avenue, Chicago, IL 60601

Jepson-Murray Advertising, 1116 N. Washington Avenue, Lansing, MI 48906

Johnson & Dean, Inc., Sixth Floor, Waters Building, Grand Rapids, MI 49503

Jordan/Tamraz/Caruso Advertising, 1419 N. Wells St., Chicago, IL 60610

Kauffman Stewart, 890 Butler Square West, Minneapolis, MN 55403

Keller Crescent Co., 1110 East Louisana Street, P.O. Box 3, Evansville, IN 47711

Kerker & Associates, Inc., 1000 Southgate Office Plaza, Minneapolis, MN 55437

Keroff & Rosenberg Advertising, Inc., 444 N. Wabash, Chicago, IL 60611

Ketchum/Mandabach & Simms, 111 N. Canal Street, Chicago, IL 60606

Kobs & Brady Advertising, 142 East Ontario, Chicago, IL 60611

Kolon, Bittker & Desmond, Inc., North Centre Building, Troy, MI 48083

Lacey Lamaster Nelson Farmer, Inc., 430 First Avenue North, Ste. 500, Minneapolis, MN 55401

Earle Palmer Brown/Kalamazoo, 259 E. Michigan Avenue, Ste. 409, Kalamazoo, MI 49007

Leo Burnett Company, Inc., 35 W. Wacker Drive, Chicago, IL 60601

Lessing-Flynn Advertising Co., 3106 Ingersoll Avenue, Des Moines, IA 50312

Liggett Stashower, Inc., 1228 Euclid Avenue, Cleveland, OH 44115

Lintas Campbell Ewald, 30400 Van Dyke, Warren, MI 48093

Mark Howard & Partners Advertising, 81 S. Ninth Street, Ste. 420, Minneapolis, MN 55402

Mars Advertising, 24209 Northwestern Highway, Southfield, MI 48075

McCann Erickson-Detroit, 755 West Big Beaver Road, Troy, MI 48084

Meldrum & Fewsmith, Inc., Playhouse Square Plaza, Cleveland, OH 44115

Nationwide Advertising Service, The Halle Building, Cleveland, OH 44116

Noble & Associates, 3 Corporate Center, Springfield, MO 65804

Ogilvy & Mather, 675 St. Claire, Chicago, IL 60611

Ross Roy, Inc., 100 Bloomfield Hills Parkway, Bloomfield Hills, MI 48304

Simmons, Michaelson, Zieve, Inc., 900 Wilshire Drive, #102, Troy, MI 48084

Stern Advertising, 29125 Chagrin Boulevard, Pepper Pike, OH 44122

Tatham Laird Kudner, 980 North Michigan, Chicago, IL 60611

Valentine-Radford, Inc., 1100 Commerce Towers, Kansas City, MO 64199

Vince Cullers Advertising, Inc., 676 St. Clair, Ste. 2222, Chicago, IL 60611

W. B. Doner & Company, 26711 Northwestern Highway, Southfield, MI 48075

Wyse Advertising/Cleveland, 24 Public Square, Cleveland, OH 44113

Y & R, 1 South Wacker Drive, Ste. 1800, Chicago, IL 60606

Zechman & Associates, Inc., 333 N. Michigan Avenue, Chicago, IL 60601

AGENCIES IN THE SOUTHWEST

Anderson Advertising, Inc., Anderson Executive Center, 1017 N. Main, Ste. 300, San Antonio, TX 78212

Bauerlein Inc., 650 Poydras Street, Ste. 1100, New Orleans, LA 70130

Beals Advertising Agency, Inc., 5225 North Shartel, Oklahoma City, OK 73112

Berry-Brown Advertising, Inc., 2602 McKinney Avenue, Ste. 300, Dallas, TX 75204

Black Gillock & Langberg, 5851 San Felipe, Houston, TX 77057

Bozell, 500 Bozell & Jacobs Plaza, Omaha, NE 68114

Bozell, 201 East Carpenter Freeway, Irving, TX 75261

Dally Advertising, Inc., University Centre II, 1320 S. University Drive, Ste. 501, Fort Worth, TX 76107

Debruyn/Rettig Advertising, Inc., 4487 N. Mesa, El Paso, TX 79902

Duke Unlimited Inc., One Galleria Boulevard, Ste. 1709, Metairie, LA 70001

EJL Advertising/Houston, 2121 Sage Road, Ste. 200, Houston, TX 77056

Evans/Dallas, Inc., 4131 N. Central Expressway, Ste. 510, Dallas, TX 75204

Fellers & Company, 5918 W. Courtyear Drive, 5th Fl., Austin, TX 78730

Fogarty & Klein, Inc., 3303 Louisiana, Ste. 220, Houston, TX 77006

Goodwin, Dannenbaum, Littman & Wingfield Inc., P.O. Box 770100, Houston, TX 77215

GSD&M, 1250 Capitol of Texas Highway, Ste. 400, Austin, TX 78746

Hall, Northway & Scofield Advertising, Inc., 3500 Maple Avenue, Ste. 1400, Dallas, TX 75219

Joiner, Rowland Serio & Koeppel, 2305 Cedar Springs, Ste. 450, Dallas, TX 75201

Jordan Associates, 1000 West Wilshire, Oklahoma City, OK 73113

Keller Crescent Co., P. O. Box 619028, Dallas, TX 75062

Levenson, Levenson & Hill, Inc., 5215 N. O'Connor, Ste. 1100, Irving, TX 75039

Littlefield Advertising, 2727 E. 21st Street, Ste. 600, Tulsa, OK 74114

McCann Erickson, Inc., 1360 Post Oak Boulevard, Houston, TX 77056

Rick Johnson & Company, 1120 Pennsylvania NE, Albuquerque, NM 87110

Sachnowitz & Company, Inc., 3410 West Dallas, Houston, TX 77019

Schey Advertising, 3120 Southwest Freeway, Ste. 500, Houston, TX 77098

The Atkins & Associates, Inc., 1777 N.E. Loop 410, Ste. 1100, San Antonio, TX 78217

The Bloom Agency, P.O. Box 569580, Dallas, TX 75356

The Competitive Edge, Inc., 6624 Gulton Court, NE, Albuquerque, NM 87109

The Hively Agency, Inc., 520 Post Oak Boulevard, Ste. 800, Houston, TX 77027

Tracy-Locke, Inc., 216 Sixteenth Street Mall, Ste. 720, Denver, CO 80265

Tracy-Locke, Inc., 200 Crescent Court, Dallas, TX 75201

Walter Bennett Company, 1 Galleria Tower, 13355 Noel Road, Ste. 1815, Dallas, TX 75240

AGENCIES IN THE WEST

Borders, Perrin & Norrander, 1115 First Avenue, Seattle, WA 98101

Chiat Day/Mojo, 320 Hampton Drive, Venice, CA 90291

Dailey & Associates, 3055 Wilshire Boulevard, Los Angeles, CA 90010

DDB Needham, 530 Bush Street, San Francisco, CA 94108

DDB Needham, 5900 Wilshire Boulevard, Los Angeles, CA 90036

DellaFemina Travisano, 5900 Wilshire Boulevard, Los Angeles, CA 90036

DMB&B, 6500 Wilshire Boulevard, Ste. 1000, Los Angeles, CA 94104

Elgin Syferd, 1008 Western Avenue, Seattle, WA 98104

Eisaman Johns & Laws Inc., 5700 Wilshire Boulevard, Los Angeles, CA 90036

Grey Advertising, 6100 Wilshire Boulevard, Los Angeles, CA 90048

Hal Riney & Partners, Inc., 735 Battery Street, San Francisco, CA 94111

HDM Los Angeles, Inc., 4751 Wilshire Boulevard, Los Angeles, CA 90010

J. Walter Thompson, 4 Embarcadero Center, San Francisco, CA 94111

Ketchum/Hicks & Greist, 55 Union Street, San Francisco, CA 94111

Livingston & Keye, 901 Abbot Kinney Boulevard, Venice, CA, 90291

McCann Erickson, Inc., 6420 Wilshire Boulevard, Los Angeles, CA 90048

McCann Erickson, Inc., 201 California Street, San Francisco, CA 94111

Ogilvy & Mather, 5757 Wilshire Boulevard, Los Angeles, CA 90036

Rubin Postaer & Associates, 11601 Wilshire Boulevard, Los Angeles, CA 90025

Saatchi & Saatchi Advertising, 1010 Battery South, San Francisco, CA 94111

Tracy-Locke, Inc., 12100 Wilshire Boulevard, Ste. 1800, Los Angeles, CA 90025

About the Author

Alice Whitfield writes, casts, produces, and directs award-winning comedy radio out of her Manhattan-based creative/production recording studio, Real-to-Reel Recording, Inc.

Alice starred in the original cast of the hit Off-Broadway show, "Jacques Brel Is Alive And Well And Living In Paris." She traded the theatre for a sane, secure business, advertising! She spent 3½ years writing, casting, producing, and directing radio for a major New York ad agency and won virtually every industry award.

In addition to all her commercial work, Alice co-authored and starred in the Off-Broadway musical "Ad Hock." About what else? The advertising industry.

Alice Whitfield teaches the art and the business of voice-overs out of her New York studios. She is equally at home on stage, behind the "mike," in front of the console, behind and in front of the camera, on the lecture circuit and, most recently, banging away on the word processor. *Take It From The Top!* is Alice Whitfield's first book.

Alice's son is screen actor Mitchell Whitfield who makes his home in Los Angeles, California.

Index

Abelle, Brad (actor), 133–37
Abrams-Rubaloff & Lawrence (talent
    agency), 105
Accents
    authentic vs. non-authentic, 55, 56
    dialects, 55, 56, 58, 127–28, 131–32
    disguising, 56–57
    regional, 57, 128
Acting
    business of, 80, 81, 86–87, 88–89, 117–18,
        123
    importance of, in character voices,
        114–15
    importance of, in voice-overs, 141, 150,
        153, 157
    innate ability in, 116
    techniques, 65–66
Actors, voice-over, 157. *See also* Voice-over
        business; Voice-overs
    and agents, 3, 16, 17–18, 74, 97, 107–8
    attitude at auditions, 8–9, 120
    creativity of, 83, 86, 90, 91, 137, 139,
        140–41
    definition, 1
    etiquette for, 9

inspiration, 85–86, 89
self-promotion, 10–12, 109, 111, 135,
    179
Ad agencies, 75, 7, 108, 113, 123
    concept testing, 70
    lists of, 174, 176
        in East, 182–89
        in Midwest, 195–99
        in New England, 189–90
        in Southeast, 190–95
        in Southwest, 199–201
        in West, 201–2
Adams, Mason (actor), 145, 167–72
AFTRA. *See* American Federation of
        Television and Radio Artists
Agents. *See* Commercial talent agents
Airing in test market (definition), 69
American Federation of Television and
        Radio Artists (AFTRA), 2–3, 13, 20,
        41, 107, 112, 173
Animated films, 2, 114, 164. *See also*
        Cartoons; Character voices
Animatic, 70
    definition, 69
ANN (announcer), 46

Announcer, 8, 47, 135, 150. *See also* Voice-overs
Assembling (definition), 27
Audio books, 2
Audio visual houses, 174–75
Auditions, 3–4, 5–6, 86, 88–89, 96, 105, 110, 118, 135, 150, 170–71
  appropriate dress, 38–39
  attitude at, 130–31, 142, 159, 171, 180
  etiquette of, 36–37, 133
  marking copy in, 34–35
  professionalism in, 35–36
  scheduling, 20–21, 37, 97
  sign-in sheet, 33–34
  taking direction in, 34–35
  timing in, 37–38

Beck, Jackson (actor), 145–51
Bell, Ralph (actor), 145, 152–56
Bellflower, Nellie (actor), 119–24
Bloom, J. Michael, Ltd. (talent agent), 94
Booking, 36, 140, 150
  definition, 5
  etiquette, 36–37
  notification of, 5–6
Breakdown, 50–51, 96
  definition, 3–4
Buchwald, Don, & Associates (talent agency), 102
Button (definition), 129–30
Buy for the body, the buy, 137
  definition 47–48

Cans (headsets), 42, 162
Carteris, Gabrielle (actor), 79–81
Cartoons, 2, 110, 113, 114, 165–66. *See also* Character voices
  voice classes, 115–16
Casting, 4, 75, 105–6, 112
  company, 3–4, 10, 13–14, 75, 105–6, 108
  directors, 7, 8, 9, 34, 35, 96, 102–3, 104, 112, 143, 179
    attitude toward actors, 13–14, 128–29, 153–54
    feedback for actors, 10–12, 36, 140
  lists of, 173, 175–76

talent search, 110–11
  session, 4–5, 36
Celebrity endorsements, 50, 57–58, 103
Character voices, 127, 165. *See also* Cartoons
  classes, 115–16
  Disney, 110, 112–13, 116–17, 164–65
  Hanna and Barbera, 164, 165
  Warner Brothers, 164, 165
  Warner-Spielberg, 164
Cohen, Julie (actor), 84–85
Comedy
  button (definition), 129–30
  law of threes, 129
    stand-up, 87, 91
Commercials, 61, 68–72, 85, 106, 113, 131, 135–36
  acting in, vs. theatre, 143–44
  celebrity endorsements, 51, 103
  code number, 44
  committee, 42–43, 139, 154
  cut-off date, 62
  cycle, 61, 77, 78
  fees, 19–20
  market research, 69–70
  on-camera, 77, 138, 139, 139
  pre-production, 70–71
  production costs, 71–72
  radio, 2, 68, 71
  sound effects, 45
  television, 1–2, 62, 68, 71, 72, 77, 78
  test-market, 69
Commercial talent agents, 3–4, 15–17, 61–62, 73–74, 105–6, 170,
  commission, 40–41, 72
  definition, 15–16, 102–3
  difficulty obtaining, 17–18, 100–101
  feedback for actors, 106–7
  and free-lance talent, 17–18, 74–75, 105
  learning the business, 100, 102–3
  lists of, 173–75
  problems of, 16–17, 103–4
  talent search, 97–100, 103, 106–8
Conflicts, 62, 162
Contract, 78, 96, 101, 113
  clean (definition), 96

Copy, 47, 59, 64, 120, 153
    character, 107
    definition, 5
    delivery standing, 61
    marking, 34–36, 141
    reading techniques, 63–67, 106, 126, 140,
        151, 159, 163, 166
    suitable for a voice, 26, 61, 154
    understanding, 160–61
    writers, 45, 153, 154–55
Creative director. *See* Casting, director
Credibility, 56, 57–58, 67, 96
Cut-off date (definition), 62
Cycle, of commercial, 77, 78
    definition, 61

Demo, 44, 71
    definition, 23
    sessions, 123
Demo reel, 58, 112–13, 114, 115, 117
    cost, 29–30
    definition, 6, 25
    for self-promotion, 6, 10, 75, 101, 134,
        135, 147–48, 172, 173–76, 179
    guidelines, 24–25, 29–30
    post-production, 26–28
    recording sessions, 25–26
    safety copy, 30
    selecting material, 26
    updating, 76
    use by agents, casting directors, and
        creatives, 98–99, 101, 105, 106–7,
        111, 122, 170
Dialects, 55, 56, 58, 127–28, 131–32. *See also*
        Accents
    geography in, 128
Direction, 117, 129, 155
    definition, 5
    taking, 34–35, 51–54, 55, 60, 107, 136,
        141–42, 161
Director. *See* Casting, director
Donut (definition), 46–47
Down-time (unemployment), 80, 82, 91
Dupes (definition), 31

Efx or sfx (sound effects), 46

Equalizing (EQ) (definition), 28
EQUITY (performing union), 173

Fade out (definition), 27
False start (definition), 48
Fees and wage scales, 2, 61, 72. *See also*
        Unions, performing
    casting company, 4
    holding, 77–78
    radio vs. television, 19–20
    types of fees, 19
Fyfe, Jim (actor), 90–91
Films, student, 82, 86
Financial guarantee (definition), 61
Foray, June (actor), 145, 163–67
Frame (definition), 68
Free-lance voice-over talent, 4, 74, 75, 101,
        105, 112
    definition, 3
    encouragement of, 13–14
    with foreign accents, 58–59, 101

Geographical limitation, of commercials
        (definition), 61–62
Gordon, Joyce (actor), 145, 156–63

Hard cutting (definition), 27
Headsets (cans), 42, 162
Holding fees, 77–78
Holloway, Sterling (Disney character
        voice), 114
Howell, Jeffrey D. (talent agent), 105–10

I.D.s (identifications), 25–26
Improvisation, 86, 115
Ips (definition), 29

Jargon, 47–49

Law of threes, 129
Lay it out (definition), 48
Linder, Scott S. (talent agent), 102–4
Live tag, 46
Levels, of recording, 38

Mall intercept (definition), 70
Mislove, Michael (actor), 119–24

Mixing (definition), 27
Moment before (definition), 65–66
Motivation, 65–66, 67
Mouth clicks, 41–42

Next-ons (definition), 179. *See also* Promos

Over scale (definition), 40

Peoples, Don (actor), 131–33
Perkins, Les (Disney character voices),
    110–18
Pick up (definition), 48
Plus 10 (definition), 40–41
Pre-production, of commercials
    (definition), 70–71
Producers, 36, 45, 112, 134, 137
    advertising agency, 3–4, 5, 70, 75
    demo reel, 29
    in recording session, 42–43
Promos, television, 136. *See also* Next-ons
Puts out the call (definition), 4

Radio
    actors's unions, 2–3
    spots, 46, 50, 72, 77, 139
    station announcer, 46
    writing and producing for, 31–32
Recording session, 5, 40–44, 154
    etiquette, 162
    headsets (cans), 42, 162
    in recording booth, 41–42
Recording studio, 5, 75
Recording to picture, 159, 162–63
    definition, 155
Reehling, Joyce (actor), 138–44
References and publications (agents,
    casting directors, agencies,
    production houses), 173–77
Rejection, handling, 78–79, 87, 92, 137,
    154, 166–67, 178–79
Reuse payments, 19, 61, 77
Residual payments (residual), 19, 61, 77,
    78
Right-to-work state (definition), 134

SAG. *See* Screen Actors Guild
Sarbin, Barbara (actor), 78–79
Savella, Marcia (actor), 125–31
Scale, 96. *See also* Over scale
    definition, 40
Screen Actors Guild (SAG), 2–3, 13, 20, 41,
    96, 107, 112, 156, 173
Script. *See* Copy
Sequencing, 27, 28
Session. *See* Recording session
Session fee, 19
7½ ips
    copy of radio spot, 44
    mono master, 29
    transfer of mixed audio track
        (television), 44
Sfx or efx (sound effects), 46
Shave a hair (definition), 48
Showcases, 81, 82, 83, 86, 100
Slate
    definition, 36, 48
SOT, sound on tape (definition), 47
Sound-alike, 116–17
Split the difference (definition), 47
Sternlight, Judy (actor), 86–87
Storyboard, 69, 70, 159
    definition, 68

Tag, 48. *See also* Live tag
    definition, 22, 46
Take, 36, 38, 43–44, 137, 155
    definition, 5
Take a beat (definition), 48
Take it from the top (definition), 48
Talent. *See also* Actors
    definition, 3, 77–78
Tapes. *See* Demo reel
Television. See also Commercials; Voice-
    overs
    test-market, commercials, 69
Three in a row (definition), 48
Topol, Richard (actor), 82–84
Training films, 2

Unions, performing, 2–3, 148–49, 162. *See
    also* American Federation of

Television and Radio Artists;
EQUITY; Screen Actors Guild
benefits, 22
contract negotiations, 96
non-union work, 76–77
pay scales, 40–41, 102, 148
and professionalism, 148–49, 156
right-to-work state, 134
work guidelines, 20, 34
Use fees, 19, 72

VO (voice-over), 46
Voice
age, 50, 95, 97, 103, 108–9, 128, 138
range and timbre, 12, 26, 97, 128
credibility, 56, 57–58, 63, 67, 96
mouth clicks, 41–42
natural, 113–14
nervous habits, 64
print, 114, 116–17
protection of, 161–62
speech impediments, 57
style and type of, 11–12, 26, 60–61, 103,
153
track, 136
trends, 95, 103, 104, 109, 118, 158
Voice-over business, 94
agencies, 112
audition scheduling, 20–21, 105, 106
career-building, 101–2, 178–79
classes, 58–56, 112–13, 114, 166, 170
conflicts, 62
employment opportunities, 2, 133–37,
179
engineers and microphones, 132, 155

geographical limitations, 61–62
importance of reading aloud, 125–26,
170
importance of good records, 179
job security of, 21–22
marketing trends, 95
professionalism, 144, 148–49, 158, 162,
180
sessions, 40–44
support among actors, 124, 132, 180
taking direction and criticism, 51–54,
60, 107, 141–42
terminology, 45–49
tools of the trade, 37–38
teaching, 142–43
training, 109–10, 121, 131, 132–33, 144,
162
women in, 108, 138
Voice-over tape. *See* Demo reel
Voice-overs, 28, 44, 50–51, 77, 139, 169. *See
also* Announcer
compared to on-camera, 138–39
definition, 1–2
humor in, 141–42
importance of acting skills in, 141, 150,
153, 157
jargon, 47–49
non-broadcast, 2, 179
style, 66

Weaver, Linda (talent agent), 94–102
Whitfield, Mitchell (actor), 88–89
Working to picture. *See* Recording to
picture
Writers. *See* Copy, writers